Protecting
Your Collectible
Treasures

JUDITH KATZ-SCHWARTZ

Protecting Your Collectible Treasures

Secrets of a Collecting Diva

Protecting Your Collectible Treasures: Secrets of a Collecting Diva
© 2001 by Judith Katz-Schwartz

Martingale & Company
20205 144th Avenue NE
Woodinville, WA 98072-8478 USA
www.martingale-pub.com

Printed in the United States of America
06 05 04 03 02 01   6 5 4 3 2 1

MISSION STATEMENT

We are dedicated to providing quality products and service by working together to inspire creativity and to enrich the lives we touch.

Library of Congress Cataloging-in-Publication Data available upon request.

ISBN: 1-56477-388-4

Dedication

To Arthur James Schwartz, He Who Is The Light Of My Life

Acknowledgments

MY ETERNAL GRATITUDE TO:

My husband, Arthur Schwartz, for his encouragement, wonderful sense of humor, and technical advice.

My mother, Beatrice Katz, for being impressed with everything I've ever done, no matter how faulty it really was.

My father, Mickey Katz, who thought I could do anything. That's where I got the idea!

My grandmother Celia Barchat Miller, who left me the greatest legacy of all.

My sister, Evelyn Cohen, who shouldered a substantial burden so that I could be free to write this book.

My brother, Arnie Katz, who continues to make sure my feet remain planted firmly on the ground at all times. And thanks to both my siblings for having those wonderful kids, who lend joy to my life each and every day.

David Maloney, who gave me the key.

Christopher Kuppig, who was my guide through the portal.

Mary Green, who took a big step and a big chance on me. Thanks for the continued support and encouragement.

Kathryn Conover, great editor and good shepherd, for all the late-night phone calls filled with laughter.

Stan Green, for laying it all out for me.

Tina Cook and Terry Martin, who patiently helped me through this freshman endeavor with good humor and kind ears.

Ellen and Steven Sussman, the kindest, most generous teachers ever born, who gave me a priceless education, absolutely free.

Barbara and Ron Pace, Sandi and Don Ferguson, and Phillip Rossetto, who kept the support and advice coming while I was locked away, and whose friendship enriches every day of my life.

Harrice Miller, Jane Clarke, Judi Scheele, and Isabelle Bryman, for their ceaseless cheerleading, encouragement, and steadfast devotion, way, way beyond the call of duty.

Contents

Preface · 13

How to Use This Book · 14

Toy Treatments
*Or, How to Keep Your Playthings
Moving and Looking Great*
· 15 ·

Doctoring Your Dollies · 20

Stuffed Toys · 22

Plastic Toys · 23

Tin Toys · 23

Vinyl Toys · 25

Furniture Fresheners
*Or, How to Save and Protect Your Collectible Furniture
from the Ravages of Everyday Life*
· 26 ·

Cleaning Wood Furniture · 30

Unsticking Sticky Drawers · 32

Getting Rid of That Smell · 32

Gorgeous Gleaming Glassware
*Or, How to Remove Stains, Smudges, and Dirt from
Your Glass and Crystal*
· 33 ·

Making Your Glass Glisten · 37
Mirror Magic · 37
Narrow Necks and Stubborn Stains · 37
Crystal Clear · 39

Paper Palliatives
Or, Secrets of Cleaning, Preserving, and Protecting Your Paper Collectibles
· 40 ·

The Great Soak-Off: Salvaging Victorian Scrap · 43
Murdering Mold and Mildew · 45
Caring for Paper Collectibles · 46

Metal Magic
Or, Maintaining the Beauty and Value of Aluminum, Brass, Bronze, Cast Iron, Chrome, Copper, and Pewter
· 50 ·

Removing Rust · 55
Aluminum Aid · 56
Brass Beauty · 56
Bronze · 57
Cast-Iron Cures · 57
Chrome Care · 58
Copper · 59
Pewter Pointers · 61

Stunningly Shiny Silver
Or, How to Produce and Keep That Warm Glow on Your Silver Collectibles
· 62 ·

First, Know What You Have · 67
Three Easy Ways to Clean Silver · 68
And Some Not-So-Easy Ways · 69
Eight Great Ways to Retard Tarnish · 70

Dos and Don'ts for Storing Silver · 72

Repairs · 72

Bijou Benefactors
Or, Neat Tricks for Taking Care of Your Collectible Jewelry
· 73 ·

Making Your Jewelry Sparkle · 76

Caring for Copper Jewelry · 77

Treating Corrosion or "Green Gunk" · 78

Protecting Your Pearls · 79

Replacing Rhinestones · 79

No More Tangles · 80

Porcelain Prescriptives
Or, How to Repair and Maintain Your Porcelains and Pottery
· 81 ·

Cleaning and Stain Removal · 84

Repairing Hurt Porcelains and Pottery · 85

Safe Storage · 87

Pottery Pointers · 87

Saving the Music
Or, Recommendations for Radios, Record Players, and Records
· 88 ·

TLC for Your Records · 93

Radios and Record Players · 94

Terrific Textiles
Or, Restoring the Original Splendor of Your Vintage Linens, Silks, and Rugs
· 97 ·

Lovely Linens · 102

Vintage Lace · 105

Sensational Silks · 105

Vintage Clothing · 106

Rugs and Carpets · 107

Simple Fabric Repairs · 109

Storing Your Textiles · 109

Recycling Textiles · 111

Last but Not Least
Or, Tips for Restoring and Protecting a Medley of Collectibles
· 112 ·

Dented Beer Cans · 118

Candles and Candleholders · 118

Leather Lore · 119

Marble Magic · 119

Perfect Picture Frames · 120

Plastics · 121

Recipes and Newspaper Clippings · 121

Treenware · 121

A Final Word on the Tools of the Trade · 123

About the Author · 125

Index · 127

About the Author · 125

Index · 127

Preface

So FREQUENTLY, when attending a show or an auction, a collector will happen upon a delightful piece that would make a wonderful asset to a collection, save for one thing: it's dirty or in less than perfect condition. How wonderful it would be to have a little book at home that could help you bring that almost wonderful piece up to snuff, using just what was around the house.

I wrote this book to fill that need. Compiling it was a pleasurable puzzle, and I spent many enjoyable hours deciphering the secrets of popular commercial cleaners, demystifying repair techniques, and simplifying it all for home use. There's a big plus, in my mind, to a job that can be done without the use of dangerous and environmentally unsafe chemicals.

I first began demonstrating these little tips years ago on FOX's *Personal FX: The Collectibles Show*. It soon became apparent from viewer response that people really were interested in knowing how to care for the things they loved and in getting back to the basics.

This book project also gave me the opportunity to write a few personal essays and share my memories of my eccentric but loveable family. So many of the objects that I collect are filled with rich associations because of my family's humor, love, and unique personality. I hope you'll find my words as enjoyable to read as I found them to write.

How to Use This Book

I THINK you'll find this book straightforward. Each chapter deals with a particular material (silver, glass) or collectible category (toys, jewelry). Each of the chapters begins with a topical essay, followed by tips and tricks for cleaning, repair, and maintenance. You can read this book straight through, go directly to a chapter of particular interest, or curl up with one of the essays for a few laughs. The index can help you locate specific topics.

Toy
Treatments

Or, How to Keep Your
Playthings Moving
and Looking Great

Since the beginning of time, toys and games have been an important part of daily life, and not just for children. When archeologists opened Tutankhamen's tomb and began examining the objects that were to accompany him to the afterlife, they found an essential item: a backgammon board. This makes me wonder what those ancient Egyptians could have been thinking. I mean, King Tut was only eighteen when he died. His first choice in playthings was probably a *girl!*

Toys are wonderful reflections of the society in which they exist. The Victorians considered children to be adults-in-training, so all toys were designed to teach them important skills they'd need when they were grown. That's why we see so many Victorian sets of miniature dishes and child-size cooking implements on the market. All were meant to teach young girls how to run a household someday.

The value of collectible toys can be maintained or even enhanced with careful care.

There were also "reckoning" toys such as spelling and counting boards, made to teach young Victorians the "three Rs." Some of the most elaborate and colorful board games come from the nineteenth century, and most reflect the sensibilities and surroundings of the Victorian age.

Toy cars, trucks, and planes usually look just like the ones on the road during the decade in which they were made, which makes them easier to date than some other objects. Other toys have trademarks, enabling collectors to identify not just the country of origin and the maker, but a toy's age as well.

The materials from which they are made can help the collector date other toys and games. For instance, toys manufactured during World War II were almost always made of paper or plastic, because rubber and many metals were unavailable to toy manufacturers during the war.

As the Industrial Revolution unfolded in the late nineteenth and early twentieth centuries, toymaking changed, along with almost every other aspect of life. As the production of handmade toys declined and mass production boomed, toys were placed into the hands of many children who had never had any but the most rudimentary playthings before. Little girls who had never owned a doll more elaborate than a rolled-up rag with yarn for hair could now play with beautiful, lifelike dolls that wore fashionable wigs, clothing, and accessories.

Now that everyone could afford a wonderful manufactured toy, handmade objects became scarcer. Eventually, handmade toys, instead of residing at the low end of the scale, came to be considered a luxury. The perception that handmade toys are more special than mass-produced ones has endured to this day.

Perhaps that's the reason my brother, Arnie, decided, when he was about eight years old, to make his own toy. He did it by stuffing his own clothes with newspapers—using a stuffed paper bag with a Halloween mask on the front as a head—and adding a baseball cap on top. Arnie left the life-size doll sitting in the chair in his bedroom. At first glance, you'd swear it was Arnie sitting there. Every single member of the family walked into that room and began talking to the doll before realizing that it wasn't Arnie. Arnie found this hysterically funny, each and every time it happened, although the joke got pretty old, pretty fast for the rest of us.

One day, Arnie—ever the creative type—decided it was time to do more than just leave his big doll on the chair waiting around for some hapless yutz to come and talk to it. He hung the doll in the window of his room, suspending it by the venetian blind cord. I suppose this met with dim acceptance, if not approval, from the rest of us, because we stopped mistaking it for him all the time and there was now a place to sit down in his tiny room. After a couple of days, he lost interest in the Arnie dummy and turned his attention to his other great love: Zorro. Donning his black gaucho hat, worn even with his pajamas, Arnie endlessly sang the theme song from the *Zorro* television series. If you've ever experienced Chinese water torture, you'll know what this was like for the rest of us.

One afternoon Mom was just sitting down to a cup of coffee, something that rarely happened—Mom sitting down, I mean. The moment she was settled at the kitchen table, the phone rang. Mom went to the telephone table in the hallway and picked up the phone. It was a neighbor, someone who lived on the next block.

"Mrs. Katz," the caller said, "you don't really know me. Our backyards face each other. Mrs. Katz, I need you to sit down now. I have something awful to tell you, something terrible."

Mom couldn't imagine what could have happened that was terrible enough to cause a neighbor she didn't even know to phone her. Maybe there hadn't been any trash collection that day and someone's dog had dumped garbage all over the street. Maybe a manhole cover had blown off on the next block and there was a big hole in the ground. Maybe, God forbid, the milkman had left a note that there was a problem in the factory and there'd be no cream cheese for a week. This would really have been a tragedy because, at the time, my brother existed solely on cream cheese and jelly on white bread, and he was much too skinny already. Mom obediently sat down, shushing Arnie, who was singing in the living room at the top of his lungs.

"Mrs. Katz," the voice at the other end of the phone shrieked hysterically, "I'm afraid your son has killed himself!" Mom looked across the room at Arnie, babbling away about "the fox that's known as Zorro," and was about to tell the caller she had the wrong house, when it all started coming together for her.

"What are you talking about?" she asked as she glared in Arnie's direction.

"I'm afraid your little boy has hanged himself—accidentally, of course. I glanced out my kitchen window and I can see into the window of his room and—Mrs. Katz, I'm so sorry, so very sorry."

Mom did her best to calm down the sobbing woman, hung up the phone, and beckoned to Arnie.

"Get that doll out of the window right now! Immediately! I want those clothes in the hamper in five minutes and don't forget to throw every bit of that newspaper in the garbage!"

Zorro reluctantly trudged into his room, released the "victim" from his venetian blind–induced bondage, removed the mask and cap, tied a knot in the paper bag, and jumped on it as hard as he could. The resulting loud pop resounded through the house, marking the death of the life-size puppet as well as my brother's brief career as a toymaker.

For today's toy collectors, it's not uncommon to come across a desired object at a flea market or antiques show that is in almost but not quite perfect condition. Collectors who know they can take the toy home and improve it are ahead of the game. With a minimum of effort, using just what you have around the house, you can upgrade the condition and appearance of almost any toy.

Doctoring Your Dollies

Cleaning Away Grit and Grime

- **Porcelain and Bisque Dolls.** Most porcelain and bisque (unglazed porcelain) dolls will clean up very nicely with tepid water and ordinary soap. Be careful not to drip any water into the eye sockets, or you'll soften them. If you're cleaning a doll that's really filthy, use acne soap. Milk, applied with a soft cotton pad, works well also.

This bisque doll has been thoroughly cleaned and is now ready for simple repair.

- **Composition Dolls.** Use cold cream, waterless facial cleanser, or another oily cleaner. Apply gently with a damp cloth. You can also use Jubilee kitchen wax on a cotton swab or Vaseline Intensive Care lotion with a damp cloth.

- **Vinyl Dolls.** For vinyl dolls that are dirty (not stained, just showing surface dirt), an acne medication such as Clearasil works very well as a cleaner. Leave it on for half an hour, longer if the surface is exceptionally filthy. Then wash it off with a soft cloth and tepid water. Milk or rubbing alcohol also works, and both will remove ballpoint-pen ink. If the doll is moldy, apply solid vegetable shortening, leave the doll in the sun for a day, and then wipe off.

- **Hard Plastic Dolls.** A chlorine-free bathroom cleaner such as Soft Scrub will do the trick. Apply a small amount to a soft damp cloth and gently rub it on the doll. Jubilee kitchen wax and Liquid Wrench also clean plastic dolls.

- **Barbie Dolls.** While Barbies are usually made of vinyl or hard plastic, they have unique problems. Many early Barbie dolls have green ears from the corroded metal in their pierced earrings. Remove the earrings, then apply Clearasil StayClear Clearstick Maximum Strength medication to Barbie's ears with cotton balls, leaving the cotton stuck to her head. Cover the head with plastic wrap, or seal Barbie in a covered dish, and let her sit that way for at least four days. Remove the covering and the cotton, carefully rinse Barbie's ears, and dry thoroughly. If your Barbie has a vinyl face or body, clean it with rubbing alcohol. To clean her arms and legs, use acetone-based nail-polish remover (not the acetone-free kind) on a cotton swab.

Restoring Hairdos

To restore the shine to your doll's wig, rub a little Johnson's baby oil into the palms of your hands, then stroke the doll's hair. Comb or brush through for a nice shine. Good for your hands, too!

If you need to glue a doll's wig back on, use rubber cement. It will enable you to remove the wig later, if necessary, without damaging the doll.

Doll Clothing and Accessories

Don't attempt to wash fragile doll items, like silk flowers or clothing. Instead, fill a paper or plastic bag with approximately ½ cup of ordinary table salt. Drop the item into the bag, close the bag, and gently shake a few times.

Remove the item, which will now be a lot cleaner and brighter. Small dolls can also be cleaned this way. The salt can be reused for this purpose—but not for cooking or eating.

Making Repairs

A doll's broken joints can be glued and painted over. Use epoxy, or mix denture powder with an all-purpose glue until you get a sticky mixture, thin enough to spread but not runny. Apply the glue, match up the two pieces, and secure with a clamp. Allow the joint to dry thoroughly, then paint to match the rest of the doll. I like acrylic craft paints best, but almost any kind of paint will do.

Storage

Never store dolls in plastic bags. Wrap them in tissue paper, place in a box, and store in a cool, dry place. Sleep-eye dolls should be stored facedown.

Ordinary baking soda can be used to clean your stuffed animals.

STUFFED TOYS

STUFFED TOYS can easily be made clean and dust-free. Put the toy into a zipper-lock bag. Add approximately 1 cup of baking soda. Seal the bag and shake it a few times. Remove the toy, and brush off or vacuum the excess baking soda.

To sanitize stuffed animals and keep them from being invaded by dust mites, seal the toy(s) in a plastic bag or plastic wrap and place in your freezer for 24 hours. The freezing temperature will kill any dust mites present, along with their eggs.

Plastic Toys

To CLEAN plastic toys, use this home recipe:

Make a paste of ½ cup baking soda and 2 or 3 tablespoons of liquid dishwashing soap. Use a toothbrush to rub the mixture onto the toy. Rinse and dry thoroughly.

Tin Toys

WHETHER YOU have windup or battery-operated tin toys, you can improve their appearance immensely by removing rust, cleaning them thoroughly, and then protecting them from contact with the air to prevent further rusting.

Removing Rust

Apply ketchup to the rusty spots, being careful *not* to get it on paint that is intact. A cotton swab is useful for getting the ketchup into small areas and directing it precisely where you want it. Let stand for 20 minutes. Wipe the ketchup off, being careful not to smear it.

Whether or not to touch up the paint is a personal decision. If I expect a toy to remain in my collection and the formerly rusty spot (which will now be black) is in a visible place, I'll repaint it. I prefer paint pens, available at any art and craft supply store. Do be aware that should you ever wish to sell such a toy, repainting may lower its value. You should always disclose any alterations to potential purchasers.

Cleaning Up

Once the rust is removed, it's time to clean off the surface dirt. Add some mild dishwashing liquid to warm water and swish it around to make suds. Use a damp sponge to wipe the solution on your toy. Use a separate sponge with clean, tepid water to rinse off the soap,

The Skating Waiter shown here looks great and is protected from rust by a coat of paste wax.

and then dry with a towel. To ensure that the toy is completely dry, follow up by blow-drying on the lowest setting.

To protect your treasure from further rust, you'll need to provide a barrier between the tin and the air. Use clear paste wax. Apply a thin coat of wax with a clean rag or sock. Wait exactly 20 minutes, then vigorously buff the toy with another clean rag or sock. You'll bring up a high shine, and your toy will look great.

Making Repairs

Windup toys are very difficult to repair because there are so many delicate moving parts. If you bought a windup toy that wasn't working, I hope you paid only a few dollars for it. If it's not a particularly rare toy, you may want to use it as an educational tool. Pry up the little tabs that hold the two halves together. Do this carefully, because they break easily. By looking inside, you can learn how the spring works.

If the toy isn't working, you'll probably find one of two things wrong: either the parts have rusted solid or there is a broken part, most likely the spring. You can try the ketchup method (page 23) on rusted parts, or you can soak them in vinegar for an hour. If the spring is broken, it must be replaced. There's no way to repair it.

Battery-operated toys are far easier to repair than windups. That's because these toys are powered not by a spring mechanism but by electricity. The slightest loss of contact with the battery electrode will stop the toy. Sometimes, all that's needed is a good shake or a firm tap on the bottom to reestablish the contact. If this doesn't work, open the battery compartment, remove the batteries, and check the battery contacts for rust. Use steel wool or the ketchup method to clean off the rust. Dry the contacts completely before reinserting the batteries. The vast majority of battery-operated toys need no more repair than this.

Toys that don't work should be bought for parts or for display only. This nonworking Charlie McCarthy was purchased for $5.

Vinyl Toys

To CLEAN vinyl toys, use full-strength baking soda on a damp sponge. Rub all over, rinse, and dry.

If a vinyl toy is moldy, apply solid vegetable shortening. Leave the toy in the sun for a day; then wipe off the shortening.

Furniture
Fresheners

Or, How to Save and Protect

Your Collectible Furniture from the

Ravages of Everyday Life

Years ago, I visited a fascinating exhibition at the Cooper-Hewitt Museum in New York City called "Now I Lay Me Down to Eat." The exhibit, which featured various now-defunct implements of basic life, included numerous paintings depicting the Last Supper as a meal which everyone ate while lying down. I had always thought the reason was that the Last Supper was a Passover Seder, a meal that Jewish men eat while reclining.

The exhibit's display of various neck rests—apparently a standard piece of dining furniture during ancient times—suggested otherwise. Evidently, people didn't sit in chairs for meals, possibly because there were no chairs. They actually ate lying down, while their necks rested on these objects that resembled slingshots. I

Fine antique furniture deserves gentle and thorough care.

thought at the time that it was a very interesting way to eat, but now I think it must also have served as a form of population control, since a substantial number of people must surely have choked on their food. The Heimlich maneuver was, of course, centuries in the future.

The exhibit's most impressive aspect, for me, was the stark contrast between life then and life now, all based on the fact that there was no furniture as we know it. There were no tables, no chairs, no sofas, no beds, no desks. People sat on natural outcroppings of stone or squatted in the dirt to converse. They sat on the ground to eat, or reclined at formal dinners. The few folks who could read or write really didn't have the space or the materials with which to do it. Most news and information was passed verbally from person to person.

I know what you're thinking. What about the Egyptians and papyrus and all the gorgeous lounges and tables the pharaohs had?

I don't know about you, but I can think of better sources for my historical references than Paramount Pictures. Papyrus was a material available to royal scribes, used mainly for royal decrees. Even hieroglyphics were most often written on walls, not paper (talk about your graffiti!). And the thrones in which you see the pharaohs seated were the only chairs in the kingdom.

So I think it's safe to conclude that furniture as we know it is not an ancient thing, at least not for the common man. As furniture did come into use, it served many different roles. Special portable campaign furniture, some of it quite elaborate, was created for generals to take to war. (Generals were never expected to be in a situation that might damage their property.)

There's a famous story about Queen Victoria and furniture. It seems that Her Majesty, when she was in her late seventies, was hosting a little family get-together at the castle (oh, say, fifty relatives or so, nothing unmanageable). She had been strolling around the room, probably checking to see that everyone was still wearing black thirty years after Prince Albert died. When she returned to her place at the head of the table, a young prankster who was either mentally disabled or had no will to live pulled the queen's chair out from under her just as she was sitting down, causing her to land, with an enormous thud, on the floor.

Numerous footmen, butlers, male relatives, stable boys, doctors, chimney sweeps, security men, and passersby rushed over to lift the queen, slowly, and place her safely into her chair. Apparently, the power winch had not yet been invented. The queen, the story goes, without ever changing her facial expression (as if she had any), looked the budding royal comedian in the eye and said, "We are not amused." Guess she cut *his* stand-up comedy career off before it got started!

To many beginning collectors, the word *antiques* translates as *furniture*. People who haven't yet become accumulators and haven't been exposed to the vast array of things collectible think that when you go antiquing, you're looking for chairs, a lamp, or an end table. Collectors who don't own enormous homes or deep pockets know different. Still, many of us own a few pieces of antique furniture, and whether you're actually collecting it or just sitting on it, knowing how to keep your furniture looking great is a worthwhile skill.

CLEANING WOOD FURNITURE

WHEN YOU buy an old grimy piece of furniture, don't rush to strip the finish off. Sometimes all that's needed is a thorough cleaning. Waterless hand cleaner, available in any hardware store, is great for lifting grease and grime off wood furniture. Once you've removed all the dirt, it's time to tackle specific problems.

Removing Wax

If someone (perhaps you) has dripped candle wax on your fine wood furniture, freeze the wax with an ice cube. You will then be able to pop it off in one piece, using a credit card, plastic scraper, or putty knife. If the wax doesn't come off in one piece, then it wasn't completely frozen. (Try the same trick to remove old chewing gum stuck underneath a desk or table. The older the gum, the better it works.)

You can also try the opposite approach. Use a blow dryer to soften and melt the wax, and then scrape off the residue.

Banishing Crayon Marks

If your kids decided to redecorate your furniture with crayon, put acetone-based nail-polish remover on a clean cloth and rub lightly on the wood to remove it.

Paper stuck to furniture is easily and safely removable.

Removing Stuck-on Paper

Saturate the paper with a few drops of olive oil. After it soaks through, rub gently with a soft cloth. Remove the paper.

To remove glue residue left by a price sticker, try lighter fluid (not butane) or peanut butter.

Removing Those Nasty White Water Rings

When guests put their wet glasses on your furniture, there are several remedies you can try.

- **Toothpaste.** Put a dab of toothpaste on a soft cloth. Rub in a circular motion until the ring disappears. A mixture of half toothpaste and half mayonnaise also does the trick.

- **Mayonnaise.** Straight mayonnaise will work if you rub it onto the mark and leave it on overnight. In the morning, wipe it off. The ring should be gone.

- **Cigar Ashes.** Cigar ashes mixed with mayonnaise, then rubbed onto the stain, is another effective method.

- **Gentle Heat.** Place blotter paper over the ring and iron with a warm (not hot) iron. If this doesn't work the first time, rub the stain with lemon oil, reapply the paper, and iron again.

Removing Glue

If your little ones get model glue on the furniture, rub on cold cream, peanut butter, or salad oil with a soft cloth.

Removing Fingerprints

Rub your fingerprinted furniture with a clean cloth saturated in olive oil.

Unsticking Sticky Drawers

Apply soap or wax to make sticky drawers glide easily.

REMOVE THE drawer from the piece of furniture and empty out the contents. Turn the drawer over and put it on a flat surface. Rub a candle, paraffin block, or bar of soap along the sides where the drawer makes contact with the runners in the piece of furniture.

Getting Rid of That Smell

MUSTY ODORS are especially offensive inside drawers and cupboards. Place unused ground coffee in a small, open container and put it inside the drawers or at the bottom of a cupboard, or simply throw a fabric softener sheet inside. After a few days, it will smell great in there!

If the inside of your cupboard has a strong paint smell, put a sliced onion inside for a few hours. It will absorb the paint odor. Trust me on this one.

Gorgeous Gleaming Glassware

Or, How to Remove Stains, Smudges, and Dirt from Your Glass and Crystal

R are is the household that doesn't have some mismatched glassware, stained vases, chipped ashtrays, or drinking glasses that started out life as something else. My grandmother was famous for this, at least in our family, because she was the Empress of Never Throwing Anything Away. So she had quite an assortment of jelly jars, peanut-butter jars, pickled-herring jars, and yahrtzeit glasses, all pressed into service as drinking vessels, flower holders, denture soakers, plant waterers, and containers for everything from buttons to bobbins.

Many of the problems that mar beautiful glassware can be solved at home.

Grandma never met an empty jar she didn't like. It always amazed me that she could remove every trace of the jar's previous life, at least in her own mind, and then use it for a completely unrelated purpose. She'd use a coffee jar to hold laundry detergent, and there wasn't even the slightest whiff of coffee smell in it. She could placidly sip tea from a jar, with a sugar cube clenched in her teeth Russian-style, confident that not a trace remained of the Murphy's oil soap that was its previous tenant. Of course, sometimes she reused jars and didn't let us know she had changed the contents. That's how we ended up, one Passover, eating spinach balls fried in dishwashing detergent. But that's another story.

What I found most unnerving were the yahrtzeit glasses. Yahrtzeit are glasses filled with candles that are burned in honor of dead relatives, usually on the anniversary of their deaths and also on Yom Kippur, the Jewish Day of Atonement. Since Grandma had lost a large chunk of her family to the Cossacks, her tray full of yahrtzeit glasses was like a miniature chandelier. When she got all the candles lighted, no other illumination was necessary in the room. When they all burned out, she'd scrape out the leftover wax, clean up the glasses until they sparkled, and put them in her cupboard, along with the 4,000 other yahrtzeit glasses already in there.

One day, I came by Grandma's apartment to pick her up for one of those grand adventures every outing with Grandma inevitably became and found the table set for breakfast. This wasn't unusual. No one was allowed out of Grandma's apartment for any reason without first sitting down to consume massive quantities of whatever she commanded one to eat. Because I am so much like Grandma, I immediately objected, even though I was well aware from previous experience that my protests would be futile.

"Grandma," I said, "I just ate breakfast."

"So, you'll have lunch."

"It's 10:30 in the morning, Grandma. It's too early for lunch. And who eats eggs and bagels and peanut butter and cream cheese and jelly and orange juice and milk and pickled herring and lox and baked salmon for lunch?"

With a straight face, Grandma replied, "Vaht, the police vill come and take you to jail if you eat dot for lunch?"

The usual back-and-forth ensued, followed by the realization that I wasn't going to win (I never did), followed by my being seated at the table, where I noticed that the orange juice was in a yahrtzeit glass. I immediately stood up, glass in hand, and went to the kitchen cabinet, where I began pushing aside scores of yahrtzeit glasses in a vain attempt to find a glass that was *not* a yahrtzeit glass. Grandma came up behind me.

"Vaht?" More of a command than a question.

"I don't want to drink from one of these," I retorted. "I'm getting another glass."

"*Luzzem!*"

Uh-oh. When Grandma said "*Luzzem,*" which is Yiddish for "Leave it!," you immediately stopped whatever you were doing. That is, if you wished to live another day. I remember in grammar school, when there was chaos in the schoolyard at lunchtime, the Head Monitor (the tallest girl in sixth grade) attempted to restore order by ringing a giant brass school bell. When that bell sounded, everyone was supposed to freeze in midstep and remain perfectly silent. I always felt that the same effect could be accomplished much more efficiently by driving over to Grandma's, picking her up, and bringing her back to the schoolyard, where she would simply say, "*Luzzem.*" Kids in schoolyards miles away would stop in their tracks, not even knowing why, confused victims of the long-distance "*luzzem*" of my grandmother.

"Listen, Grandma," I mumbled, retracting my hand quickly, as if there had been a small fire in the cupboard. "These glasses are creepy. They're memorial glasses. I don't want to drink from them."

"So vaht den, from your own family you vooden drink?"

Once it becomes a matter of family loyalty, objections collapse under the burden of guilt with which they're laden. I drank the juice from the yahrtzeit glass.

Still, not even Grandma's "*luzzem*" could have convinced me to drink from a glass that hadn't been immaculate. Grandma had some mighty effective ways of restoring the sparkle to glass, and in my travels through the collecting world I've picked up a few more.

Making Your Glass Glisten

THERE ARE several good methods to achieve superclean glass. Both ammonia and vinegar will give your glass collectibles an amazing shine, free of streaks. Wipe the glass with newspaper instead of cloth, which leaves behind lint.

Another excellent glass cleaner is made by dissolving ¼ cup of cornstarch in 1 quart of warm water. Use a sponge saturated with this solution to clean your glass items. Wipe them dry with paper towels.

Rubbing alcohol also makes a great glass cleaner. You can even use vodka in a pinch.

Mirror Magic

CLEAN YOUR mirrors with Barbasol shaving cream. They won't fog, no matter how hot or damp the room gets.

Get the filth off an old mirror with Coca-Cola. Just wipe it on, and wipe it off.

Narrow Necks and Stubborn Stains

HERE ARE four techniques for removing cloudy rings and other stubborn stains from narrow-necked vases, cruets, and bottles. Hard-water marks from water allowed to stand in a vase for a long time are extremely difficult to remove—you may have to try more than one method. If the vase or bottle has been "etched," the ring will *never* come off. The following are safe for all your utilitarian and art glass.

- **The Eggshell Method.** Break up a few eggshells into small pieces. Fill the vase (or other container) about halfway with hot water, and add the eggshells. Cover the opening of the vase and shake vigorously. The eggshells will mildly abrade the glass, dislodging residue in the narrow neck.

- **The Rice Method.** Use raw rice, sliding it a little at a time into the neck of the bottle. Add hot water, cover the opening of the vase, and shake vigorously. Other small abrasives, such as sand or BBs, can be used in lieu of rice.

- **Toilet Bowl Cleaner.** Fill the vase or bottle with water and add toilet bowl cleaner according to the strength recommendations on the package. Let it stand for a couple of hours. Rinse thoroughly.

- **Denture Cleaner.** Fill the vase or bottle with hot water and drop in the denture tablet or powder. Allow to stand overnight, then rinse.

Eggshells, rice, and sand are all excellent abrasives for cleaning a glass vase with a narrow neck.

CRYSTAL CLEAR

CLEANING AN antique crystal chandelier is scary and next to impossible, you say?

Not at all! You don't even have to take down the chandelier. You do have to put a drop cloth on the floor underneath it, though. Then fill a large tumbler or wide-mouth jar with 3 parts rubbing alcohol to 1 part water. If you have no rubbing alcohol in the house, you can substitute vodka. Hold the tumbler up to each pendant to immerse it in the alcohol solution. A moment is usually all it takes. Remove the tumbler and the pendant will drip-dry, streak-free!

For pendants you can't reach with the tumbler, put on a cotton glove (or slip a sock over one hand), dip the gloved hand in the alcohol solution, and wipe each pendant.

To clean and polish fine crystal, use the same alcohol mixture or make a paste of dry mustard and distilled water (avoid tap water; it contains chemicals and minerals that can leave a residue on glass). The mustard paste is a very mild abrasive, safe for use on crystal. Wipe carefully with a damp cloth, and dry thoroughly.

Paper

Palliatives

Or, Secrets of Cleaning, Preserving, and Protecting Your Paper Collectibles

I t seems that whenever someone is trying to sell you an item older than, say, something made this morning, he tells you, "This is a Victorian piece." Sometimes he's actually correct; Victoria was queen for so long, there's almost seventy-five years' worth of paper out there that actually *is* Victorian. I think I'd know it was time to retire from my job if people had begun to name an era after me, wouldn't you? Not Victoria Regina.

Victoria wasn't even supposed to be queen, but then all those relatives between her and the throne just bit the dust, one after the other. And what an overbearing mother she had! Victoria's mom wasn't going to let the future queen of England grow up wild, so she

More collectors are discovering the beauty and content of vintage paper collectibles.

kept her daughter close—really close. Which is why, when Victoria became queen at eighteen, the first thing she did was demand a room of her own.

It was love at first sight for Victoria when she met Prince Albert, who happened to be her first cousin. Apparently, European royals hadn't yet grasped the concept of marrying *outside* the family. Victoria was obsessed with Albert and the feeling was probably mutual, because they gave birth to nine children and the Victoria and Albert Museum. They had, the story goes, a mechanism installed in the royal bedchamber whereby they pulled a lever and the children were instantly locked in their own bedrooms for the night, conveniently providing privacy for their parents down the hall.

After Albert died, Victoria went into mourning for nearly the rest of her life, taking the entire royal court with her. Ladies were forced to dress in black from head to toe, and the fad for mourning jewelry began. Talk about not going on with your life!

One thing Albert did for Victoria was encourage her to speak out, to express her opinions on politics and government. She became quite the royal battle-ax (if you've ever seen a portrait of her, you know what I mean; Her Majesty was not a "10"). I suppose a person can't help but feel powerful when she refers to herself as "we" all the time.

With the outspoken Victoria as their example, you'd think the women of England would have been independent, opinionated, and politically involved. In reality, they were consumed with such intellectually challenging pursuits as lecturing the servants, devising complicated rules for the leaving of calling cards at each other's homes, and making jewelry out of hair.

They also compiled scrapbooks. These weren't anything like the scrapbooks we have now, composed of personal mementos and souvenirs. They consisted of endless pages of teeny, tiny little cutouts, glued on randomly or in rows. These cutouts came from advertising trade cards, from publications, and from large sheets produced solely for the purpose of having some woman sit in her parlor with a pair of scissors and snip, snip, snip for hours. Some cutouts, or *scraps* as they were called, were just ¼" in diameter. I don't know what possessed Victorian women (maybe a form of mass hypnosis?) to carefully trim around all those itty-bitty images, paste them into books, and then put them away. Because nobody was interested in these scrapbooks. Nobody. Except, of course, you and me!

We like the teeny tiny cutouts because they are colorful, pretty examples of Victorian-era graphics and illustration, and they make great display items. What we don't like is the crumbling brown pages to which they are affixed. That's why I'll tell you how to get them off those crumbling pages. And, while we're on the subject, I'll give you a few other tricks to help your paper collectibles look bright and new, instead of as old as the Queen Mum.

THE GREAT SOAK-OFF: SALVAGING VICTORIAN SCRAP

THIS IS a project for a Saturday, a day when you're not expecting any visitors, because your kitchen sink and counters will be unusable for the whole day. Once you fill the sink with water and throw in those pages, forget about preparing any food. Which, in my mind, is a plus. When I don't feel like cooking, I just fill up the sink, throw in some scrapbook pages, and tell He Who Is The Light Of My Life to take me out for lunch. If he looks curious about this request, I simply say, "The kitchen sink . . ." That's all that's necessary. HWITLOML has never even *seen* the inside of the kitchen sink, much less used it for anything. So he doesn't want

Victorian scrap, once the hobby of nineteenth-century ladies, now attracts collectors.

to know what horrible atrocity is taking place in there. So dress for your favorite restaurant, fill the sink, and begin the Great Soak-Off.

1. Fill the sink with tepid water.

2. Put the page from which you're trying to soak the scrap into the sink. If you're doing a whole scrapbook, you can put several pages in at once.

3. Go away.

4. Check back once every hour or so. Items that have come off the pages will be floating around in the sink. Take them out.

5. Continue removing pieces from the sink as they come off the page. Place them on a flat surface between sheets of paper

towels. Weight with a heavy object, such as a doorstop or platter—or a doorstop on top of a platter.

6. Change the paper towels frequently, always weighting the items so they won't curl. This process will take a couple of days, maybe longer, but won't require your constant attention. You just need to check on your items once or twice a day. The paper towels can be dried and reused.

7. When the scrap feels completely dry, put it between the pages of your heaviest book (an unabridged dictionary is great for this) and leave for a week or so.

This method works well for Victorian scrap and advertising trade cards. Don't try it with thicker items, such as baseball cards, greeting cards, or postcards. *Never*, ever, soak photographs.

MURDERING MOLD AND MILDEW

MOLD AND mildew are living organisms. Those of us who are allergic to them have a built-in mold/mildew detector. It's called a nose. We sneeze the moment we walk into a room where mold and mildew are present. This is because of the spores they release into the air. Mold and mildew need two conditions to grow into more mold and mildew: a damp environment and poor air circulation. That's why basements always smell so funky.

Mold and mildew can be easily recognized as a gray or black, sometimes fuzzy, coating with a distinctive "fragrance." They are living organisms, which means they can die. And I am proud to consider myself an expert executioner of mold and mildew.

Paper, a favorite victim of mold and mildew, is highly susceptible to damp conditions in general. In fact, a good rule to remember is this: Water is the Enemy of Paper. It behooves us all to fight that murderous mildew, that miserable mold, and protect our poor defenseless paper collectibles.

The microwave oven is a marvelous weapon in the war on mold and mildew. It not only kills them both, it also kills bugs living in your books. It will not, however, remove the gray and black stains left behind. So if you've allowed your paper things to develop that awful black stuff, it's really much too late. (You can try brushing the yucky stuff off with a soft brush, but what your papers really need at that point is a decent cremation or recycling.)

1. Place your book, paper, or postcard in the microwave oven.

2. Set the microwave on medium power and run it for 10 seconds.

3. After the microwave goes "ding," take out the paper and sniff it. If it still smells moldy, put it back in the oven and try increasing the cooking time. Remember, every microwave oven is different, so there's no magic recipe for this. It's a trial-and-error thing.

If you have paper collectibles that have acquired a musty odor but are not mildewed, let's get rid of that smell. Put them in a box with a lid, add a fabric softener sheet, and cover the box. Voilà! The standard "voilà" time is overnight, but some things take longer.

CARING FOR PAPER COLLECTIBLES

WHEN IT comes to condition, paper collectors are especially demanding. They know that very few collectibles are one of a kind, so, like many collectors, they bypass items in less-than-perfect condition, preferring to wait and purchase better examples.

I always advise new collectors to buy items in the best condition they can afford. If you purchase a paper item that's pretty nice, but not perfect, there are several things you can do to improve its appearance, and therefore its condition. And there are a number of preventive steps you can take to protect all your paper collectibles, preserving them in the condition in which they were acquired.

Cleaning and Handling

Wash your hands before handling your paper collectibles. And then dry them. Thoroughly (remember, Water is the Enemy of Paper). You may even want to wear white cotton gloves, available at any drugstore, when handling old paper. Some collectors never handle any paper without their gloves.

How you clean surface dirt from a paper item depends on its finish. Here are two options:

- **Shiny Surface.** Clean paper items with coated or shiny surfaces, like some postcards or greeting cards, with white bread. Cut off the crusts (just like Mom did for you), scrunch up the bread with your hand, and rub it on the paper. It will pick up the surface dirt.

- **Matte Surface.** For other paper items, try cleaning dirt off with cornstarch or talcum powder. Sprinkle it on, let it sit for a while, and then brush it off.

Cornstarch is excellent for cleaning a vintage valentine.

You can sometimes get wrinkles out of paper by ironing it. Heat the iron to a cool setting. Turn the paper over and iron the back of it. Keep the iron moving, or you'll leave a scorch mark.

Removing Foreign Objects

If any metal objects—staples, paper clips, pins—are in contact with your paper collectible, gently remove them. Eventually they're going to rust and leave a permanent stain.

Now, to deal with a pet peeve of mine. Dealers in antiques shops sometimes slap a price sticker right on a paper item! Now, how are you supposed to display an item with a sticker right on the front, and how are you going to remove it without pulling off part of your collectible with it? Aha! Grab a can of lighter fluid. If you still allow anyone to smoke in your household, it'll probably be sitting on a shelf somewhere. If not, any newsstand or housewares store will have it. *Note that it must be regular lighter fluid, not butane.*

Place the paper on a clean, flat surface, such as your kitchen counter. Saturate the price tag with lighter fluid. Count to five slowly, then peel off the sticker, which will come free, leaving a big oily stain on the paper. If it's a really large sticker, you may have to remove it a little bit at a time, saturating with fluid, carefully peeling, saturating, peeling a little bit more—you get the idea. While you are eyeing the oily stain left behind and thinking, "I'm going to wring that Judith's neck!," the stain will evaporate, taking with it the lighter-fluid smell. You may apologize to me now.

If the price tag has been on the paper a long time, it may leave a sticky residue. Try the talcum-powder, cornstarch, or white-bread method of removing it.

Lighter fluid also removes prices written in grease pencil by dealers who are even more insensitive than the price-tag people.

Acid-Free Display and Storage

If you're going to store or display paper items, you must protect them from coming in contact with anything that is not acid-free. It's the acid in paper that makes it turn brown, dry up, fade, and chip, so why let your collectible touch anything that will add even more acid to its environment?

Acid-free archival materials, such as backing boards and plastic sleeves, are available from mail-order suppliers, or you can purchase them in art-supply stores. Keep paper out of direct sunlight, as well as artificial light, and away from heat and humidity. If you're having a paper item framed, be sure the framer uses an acid-free mat between your treasure and the glass. The mat keeps the glass from touching the item.

Metal Magic

Or, Maintaining the Beauty
and Value of Aluminum, Brass,
Bronze, Cast Iron, Chrome,
Copper, and Pewter

You'd think it might take a genius to figure out how to clean each different type of metal and keep it looking its best. You'd also think that cleaning and maintaining all those different materials would take a large range of products and some serious elbow grease. The truth is, there are just a few basic considerations to keep in mind, and cleaning most metals is an easy job.

No one in my family would deny that my maternal grandmother was, well, unusual. At least, we didn't know anyone like her. For example, she was the most difficult shopper in the world. She drove salesmen

Most metal objects can be cared for easily and inexpensively, and some require no care at all.

crazy with her demands, making them scramble to meet her every requirement. I know for a fact that there's a shoe salesman in Brooklyn who is still taking Prozac after trying to sell her a single pair of oxfords in 1979.

"Dis is too tight," she'd say. "I vudden vear brown." "I don't like a lace mit points on it." "Dis is a heel dot looks like a man's heel."

Once, when Mom took Grandma shopping for shoes, the poor salesman had answered every objection. He had spent hours dragging boxes of shoes out of the back room until he had finally found a pair with just the right style, the right heel, the right toe box, the right laces, the right size, the right fit. It was perfect.

"Very nice," Grandma said. "I'll maybe come back next veek and buy it."

The salesman looked up at Mom and said, "Mrs. Katz, please don't bring your mother into this store again."

So, we all know Grandma could be difficult. She was also stubborn. One of the things about which Grandma was most stubborn was *her* rights in *your* home. If you left Grandma alone in your apartment, even for a few moments, you'd probably have a surprise waiting for you when you came back. You might find that suddenly your silverware drawer had been moved. She'd take everything out, clean it all, rearrange it, and then decide it should all be in the drawer on the other side of the room, so she'd move it there, and then take the stuff that had been in the other drawer and put it someplace else. Once Grandma had invaded your space, you could never find anything. And complaints were useless.

I'd say, "Grandma, don't you have any respect for my privacy?"

"From a grandma there is no privacy." And she said it with a perfectly straight face.

Admittedly, I'm a lot like her, which means I'm a stubborn person too, and I do adore a challenge. So, I resolved that I would prevent Grandma from ever again messing with my stuff. One afternoon, this resulted in a Grand Battle.

Grandma and I were alone in my apartment. She wanted to clean out my drawers.

"I'll make them nice," she said.

"Grandma, you're not touching those drawers! They're very nice the way they are."

So far, I was holding her off.

"I'll do the closets in the kitchen, then."

"You will not do the closets." (That's it, be strong, Judi.)

"*Oy*, vat is wrong mit you? Vy you are so mean? Let me help you. If you vud let me help you, I appreciate it *awful* a lot."

She was apparently trying out a new tactic, but I was too fast for her.

"Grandma, *I* would appreciate it if you *wouldn't* clean. You're a guest."

"To a grandma you say she's a guest? Oy, vaht did I do so terrible my granddaughter should hate me like poison? Let me clean your combs and hairbrushes."

Now she was really playing dirty, using the ultimate weapon: guilt. Grandma was a grand master at this, completely in control, like a mad scientist administering a new virus to a helpless victim strapped to the table in her laboratory. But I'd been vaccinated against this particular germ by a childhood full of Grandma's sly reproach. I no longer felt guilt on demand. I was immune.

"If my grandma really loved me, she'd want me to be happy. She'd let me be the hostess and wouldn't want to *work* when she came to visit."

Aha! Touché! The victim breaks out of the wrist straps, jumps off the table, grabs a sword, and is ready to duel for her life.

"Don't you know you take from me the pleasure to help you? I'll just dust the furniture."

Oh, she was tough. She had parried my perfectly coordinated thrust and lunged at me with the sword of guilt once more. I had to act fast.

"Sorry, Grandma, no dust cloths. And I just dusted before you showed up anyway."

I ignored Grandma's expression of disbelief, as she not inconspicuously ran a finger over a side table.

"How about I just straighten a little your desk?" She was undefeated. Darn! My back was pressed against the stone castle wall. But I came back.

"Grandma, don't touch my desk! You'll get me all mixed up. I know exactly where everything is right now. How will I work?"

Grandma looked around desperately. What was left that I hadn't already decreed off limits? I wouldn't let her touch anything in the kitchen, the dining room, the bedroom, or my office. I wouldn't let her fold my laundry or roll up my socks. I forbade her to clean my combs and brushes or to take all the collectibles off the shelf in one room and arrange them on top of a table in another room. She was a desperate woman. We circled each other nervously as she glanced around the room, searching for something, anything, she could clean.

At this point, nature called. I was forced to leave Grandma alone for three minutes. When I got back to the living room, there she was, victorious, dusting—you won't believe this—*the leaves on my plants* with a paper towel. She'd won again.

Lest you think there was acrimony in our frequent disagreements, let me assure you there wasn't. In my family, argument is a sport. I think we do it as a form of exercise; it keeps our minds supple or something. Rarely does an argument in my family result in hard feelings. Of course, rarely does it result in any change either. We're all great talkers, but we're not such good listeners. In fact, if you joined my family at, say, a holiday meal, you'd see what I mean. We'd all be in one room, say twenty of us, with everyone talking at once. Except not to each other. Twenty people, twenty conversations. This results in a lot of repetitious phone calls the next day, but no changes in anyone's mind, as far as I've been able to see.

So, one way or the other, Grandma always won when it came to imposing her version of order on your household. My brother, Arnie, always said, "You know, Grandma can drive you crazy, but she's excellent with pots."

He was right, of course. Grandma could take the blackest pot or pan, whether it was copper or chrome or stainless steel, work on it for a few minutes, then hand you back this gleaming vessel that you'd hardly recognize because it was so gorgeous.

She even explained her pot-cleaning technique to me, about

three trillion times at least. It's unfortunate that I failed to ever understand a single word she was saying. She'd grab a pan and a scouring pad and say, "Here, you don't do like dis," as she scoured the pot. "You just do like dis."

"Oh, I see," I'd exclaim, watching her do what looked to me like exactly the same thing she'd done the first time. So her pot-cleaning technique is lost forever (although I'll bet my sister, Evelyn, knows it).

Even though I can't share Grandma's trick with you, I have many others, all designed to keep your metal collectibles looking their very best and to help preserve their value.

REMOVING RUST

MOST METALS rust. That is a fact of metallic life. Rust is caused when the surface of the metal combines with the oxygen in the air to form iron oxide. When metal collectibles are subjected to a humid environment, they will rust faster. But don't be discouraged. Rust can be removed and its return slowed, if not prevented.

Once your items are thoroughly clean and devoid of rust (instructions for individual metals follow), store them in a closet or cabinet along with a moisture-absorbing substance such as mothballs, charcoal, chalk sticks, or cat litter. Place the material close to, but not touching, your metal objects. If you have young children or pets, choose something other than mothballs, which are poisonous.

If you're trying to get a rusted bolt or other metal part to move, soak it in Coca-Cola. If the bolt or screw remains stuck to your collectible, soak a cloth in Coca-Cola and apply it to the part for 10 minutes or so.

Knife blades with high carbon content will rust if not washed and thoroughly dried. To remove the rust, plunge the knife blade into an onion several times, then leave it in for an hour or so. The onion won't be very happy, but you will!

ALUMINUM AID

CLEANING SMALL aluminum objects, such as jewelry or ashtrays, is easy. Apply ketchup, let it sit for half an hour or so, wipe off, rinse, and dry. You can use ketchup on larger objects as well, but canned tomatoes also work and are less expensive.

BRASS BEAUTY

HERE ARE three methods for cleaning your brass collectibles:

- **Lemon Juice and Salt.** This tip is one of my all-time favorites (it also works for copper). Cut a lemon in half. Stick a fork through the skin side of one of the lemon halves to form a handle. Dip the cut side of the lemon into a dish of salt. Wipe the salted lemon all over the brass item and watch the shine appear! No pressure or elbow grease is required. Rinse in cool water and dry thoroughly.

- **Toothpaste.** Rub toothpaste on the brass with a soft cloth or toothbrush. Rinse and wipe dry.

- **Vinegar Paste.** Mix equal parts of flour and salt. Add enough vinegar to make a paste. Rub on the brass with a damp cloth. (This one also works well on copper.)

Once you have your brass items looking spiffy, give them a coat of paste wax to retard tarnish.

Bronze

Leave your bronzes alone! They should never be cleaned beyond a light dusting with a feather duster. Bronze is prized for its patina, and if you remove it, it can take a hundred years for it to come back. Also, never let your bronzes sit out in a room that is being cleaned with any product that contains chlorine.

Cast-Iron Cures

Cleaning

If you buy a cast-iron piece that's really funky, the first thing you'll want to do is get it clean. Spray it all over with oven cleaner and put it into a plastic bag. Seal or tie the bag so the cleaner won't evaporate. Let it sit for an hour or two, open the bag, and

This cast-iron ice scraper has been made free of rust.

remove the piece. You will then be able to scrub off all the crud. Use a synthetic pad, not a metal one, to avoid scratching the iron.

Preventing Rust

We all know that iron rusts as it combines with the oxygen in the air. The way to keep cast iron from rusting is to create a barrier between the iron and the air. You can do this with a coating of mineral oil.

If your item is a pot or pan that you intend to use for cooking or serving food, it is important to use *edible* mineral oil. There are two kinds of mineral oil available; one is not to be ingested by humans, so read the label to be sure you are using the right kind. Heat the pot or pan until it is warm, then rub the mineral oil on with a cloth, working it in. That's all you have to do.

To treat objects not used for food, be sure the cast iron is perfectly *dry* and *warm*. I do this with a blow dryer on the hot setting. Just aim it at the object and blow. Next, apply the mineral oil, rubbing it in well with a cloth.

CHROME CARE

Cleaning

A number of different substances can help you clean chrome in a snap. Whichever you choose, wipe it on with a soft cloth, rub gently, then rinse and dry thoroughly.

- **Turtle Wax Liquid.** Use Turtle Wax Professional Liquid Rubbing Compound. This car-care product contains a mild abrasive.

- **Rubbing Alcohol.**

- **White Vinegar.**

- **Leftover Tea.**

- **Nail-Polish Remover.**

Removing Rust and Restoring the Shine

Remove rust from chrome objects by rubbing them with a wadded-up piece of aluminum foil dipped in Coca-Cola.

To bring up a beautiful shine, make sure the chrome is absolutely dry. Then polish with—are you ready?—a fabric softener sheet.

Copper

Before using any treatment on copper, you must first determine whether or not it is lacquered. Lacquer is a clear coating, often applied when the piece is made. It prevents copper from tarnishing, but it also prevents it from acquiring a high shine. Over time, some

A toy copper stove will not tarnish because it is protected by lacquer, but it will also never achieve a high shine.

parts of the lacquer can erode. Black spots form in those areas where the lacquer is missing.

Removing Lacquer

Whether or not to remove the lacquer on a copper piece is a personal decision. I always remove it at the first sign of deterioration or if I want to use the piece for cooking or serving food. You can always relacquer your copper item later. Neither lacquer nor the lack thereof has any effect on the value of a piece.

Use nail-polish remover or its active ingredient, acetone. Acetone is a solvent that can be purchased at hardware or art-supply stores. Saturate a cloth with acetone or nail-polish remover and rub over the copper to dissolve the lacquer. Wipe off with a clean, damp cloth; wash in hot soapy water; rinse; and dry thoroughly.

Cleaning

Here are three ways to clean unlacquered copper:

- **Lemon Juice and Salt.** See the description under "Brass Beauty" (page 56).

- **Worcestershire Sauce.** Apply it straight from the bottle. Rub on with a soft brush or cloth, rinse, and dry.

- **Onions.** Boil a few onions in water. Use the water to clean copper as well as brass.

Surface Protection

If the copper items you've just cleaned will not be coming in contact with food, you can provide a protective seal to slow the tarnishing process. When the copper is perfectly dry, spray evenly with hairspray, coating it completely. Let the piece air-dry thoroughly before storing.

On the other hand, if you've purchased a reproduction piece and you'd like to give it that old green patina you see on antique copper, listen to this. Here's what the pros do to achieve that look: they bury the piece in a pile of manure for two weeks. Wear gloves, and watch where you step.

Pewter Pointers

IF YOU'RE expecting to get a high shine on your pewter antiques, forget it. It's just not going to happen. Pewter was never meant to shine but, rather, to have a warm, dull glow. Old pewter is very soft. Vigorous rubbing can cause dents or even make a hole in the pewter, so be gentle.

Incredibly Easy Cleaning

Here are three ways to clean your pewter and restore its natural glow:

- **Cabbage.** Rub your pewter with cabbage leaves. Rinse and wipe dry.

- **Wood Ashes.** Collect ashes from your fireplace and mix them with enough water to form a paste. Rub this paste on your pewter, rinse, and dry.

- **Boiling.** Put your pewter object in a pot of water, completely submerging it. Add some dishwasher detergent and bring to a boil. Turn off the heat and allow the water to cool. Remove the pewter, wash in soapy water, and polish gently with a soft cloth.

If You Simply Must Work Hard

Okay, if you're determined to make this labor-intensive, you can use a soap pad dipped in silver polish. But don't expect to get a shine. It'll just get the grime off. Rinse and thoroughly wipe dry.

Stunningly Shiny Silver

Or, How to Produce and Keep

That Warm Glow

on Your Silver Collectibles

I think we're all in agreement that there's no point in owning silver if it doesn't shine. The attractive thing about silver is the soft glow of that patina that comes with age and cleaning. But cleaning silver usually requires messy, smelly cleaners and lots of elbow grease. So, if you have silver items that are all black with tarnish, you may be tempted to get rid of them instead of tackling the daunting job of cleaning and maintaining them. You must clear that temptation out of your head.

My mom worked hard to ensure that her three children grew up to be, at the very least, polite. I'm not saying Dad didn't care about manners. We were just part of a generation that didn't turn to its dad to learn life's niceties. Dads went to work, came home,

Keeping fine silver looking beautiful need not be hard work.

sat down to read the paper, and when their offspring entered the room for the purpose of acquainting the Patriarch with something important like, say, that night's episode of *The Monkees*, said "Honey, can you get them out of here? I'm trying to read!"

Actually, I think Mom's greatest achievement in the art of child rearing was that she never strangled any of us. Instead, she reminded us endlessly, day after day, to do the things we were supposed to do, and to quit doing all those pesky other things. No singing at the table. Stop dropping apple seeds into your sister's cereal. No hair pulling, not even your own. Throw your socks in the hamper instead of on the floor. And my personal favorite: No shouting!—usually delivered at about 100 decibels.

In view of all the rules and regulations, you might expect that we were pretty timid children. You'd be wrong, of course. We were anything but timid, possibly because our memories were so short.

One Tuesday, my sister, Evelyn, and I came home from school, let ourselves into the house, and were greeted by such a major ruckus coming from the basement, it stopped us in our tracks. Ever the protective older sister, I said, "Go downstairs and find out what's going on, Ev."

Evelyn had exhibited a maternal streak almost from infancy. She used to catch frogs and name every single one of them Baby. When I first began school and had to go to bed earlier than she did (I'll bet Dad was in on that one!), she'd hear me crying myself to sleep and feel sorry for me. So she'd get her little toy baby-bottle sterilizer and fill it with pretzels, which she then heated up on the radiator in our brother's room and brought into the tiny bedroom I shared with her, saying, "Judi, I cooked you some pretzels to make you feel better." So we know she was a very kind child. She was not, however, a stupid one.

"I'm not going," she said. "You go."

We finally agreed to sit at the top of the stairs and eavesdrop on the pandemonium taking place in the basement below us.

We could recognize my mother's voice, but that other one! We couldn't even identify its gender at first. It was a screeching, high-pitched, scratchy wail. But, as we realized after a few moments, it was wailing in Yiddish, so we knew it was Grandma. She was pitching a fit, screaming at my mother about something we couldn't comprehend. One thing we did know was that there was some heavy-duty Jewish invective in there.

Jewish curses are elaborate and very succinct. If a Jew wishes you ill, you'll know it when you hear it. Evelyn and I didn't speak any Yiddish but—like everyone exposed to a foreign language on an almost daily basis—we had learned all the curses really well. At the moment, my grandmother was hoping Mom would lose all the teeth in her head except one, and in that one she was hoping Mom would have a toothache.

Mom was trying to reason with Grandma. We could tell, even though she too was speaking in Yiddish, because there were no curse words on her end of the conversation. "Mama," she kept saying, followed by Yiddish, Yiddish, and more Yiddish. Finally, we surmised that my mother had decided to go downstairs to clean out the junk in the basement and Grandma had caught her at it red-handed. Uh-oh.

Grandma's first rule of life was Never Throw Anything Away. At issue were some old pieces of silverware. I use the term *silverware* very loosely. There were coffeepots and teapots black with grime, having resided in the basement for at least twenty years. There were trays with dents and scratches and bends. There were spoons and forks with broken handles and big spots of wear.

"Mama," my mother said, "these things are just junk. They're taking up space and collecting dust." We took this lapse into English as a sign that things were calming down.

"Junk?!? *Junk!!!!*" And off Grandma went into Yiddish again, whipping herself into a fury worthy of the wildest banshee in the bunch.

As we sat there listening, a fascinating dilemma began to unfold for Evelyn and me. To our preadolescent brains, it seemed there was a protocol issue here, one that could spell opportunity for us, the residents of the lowest rung of the familial ladder.

Grandma was definitely shouting, and shouting was not allowed. In fact, extended and curse-filled shouting was a punishable offense.

Could Mom punish Grandma? Grandma was Mom's mother and, as the whole world knows, traditionally it is the moms who do the punishing. They are not the punishees. But Grandma was definitely shouting! Could punishment be enforced *up* the family ladder? As we sat and pondered, exciting possibilities presented themselves to us.

I began to feverishly concoct scenarios in my hopeful preteen head, scenarios in which the inmates were suddenly running the asylum. What could we do to provoke our mother into shouting one day, affording us the opportunity to mete out justice, to punish *her*? What would be the punishment? Would we send her to her room? Take away her TV privileges for a month (as if she ever had the time to watch TV)? We could make her stay home and watch Arnie while we went to the movies. We could *send her to bed early*. Oh, the possibilities! We strained to hear every word, as it occurred to us that the drama taking place in the basement could have important consequences for all of us. Why, it could change life for children all over the civilized world.

Of course, no punishment was meted out to Grandma (not fair, we thought!). Pretty soon, all the fuss died down. We were discovered sitting on the steps and told to stand up and get out of there because the steps were dirty. The silver went back into the dusty, musty pile at the back of the basement, and Evelyn and I went to our room to do our homework, our fleeting dreams of a secret weapon to be used in future generational combat dashed. Yes, it was, is, and shall ever be an ironclad rule: punishment is a one-way street. It is doled out in a downward direction, a direction that can never, ever, be reversed, except maybe when you grow up and go into therapy.

If I'd known then what I know now, I could have made everyone happy. There are ways of restoring even badly neglected silver to its former magnificence and keeping it that way. And that would have made both Mom and Grandma happy, although it wouldn't have done a thing for those of us in the younger generation.

First, Know What You Have

STERLING SILVER is usually marked "925" or "Sterling." This is because silver is 92.5 percent pure silver and 7.5 percent copper. Silver plate consists of a thin film of silver over copper or nickel, and will be marked "plate" or "silver plate." It's important to remember that you can't use anything abrasive or caustic to clean silver plate because the film is so thin. And *never* scour any silver, whether it's plate or sterling, with steel wool.

A sterling mark on a Victorian silver card case

Three Easy Ways to Clean Silver

The Hot-Bath Method

Use a disposable aluminum foil pan or line a plastic bowl with a piece of aluminum foil. Take off any removable parts from the silver object(s). Place the silver in a single layer on the foil. It is important that each piece of silver be touching the foil but not each other. The pieces will get much cleaner if the solution goes all around them.

Pour boiling water into the pan to cover the silver. Add 3 tablespoons or so of baking soda and 1 tablespoon salt. (Or, use Spic and Span floor cleaner instead of the soda and salt.) Wait until all the tarnish comes off. Usually, this takes about 15 minutes, but it could take much less time. You don't want to leave your silver in a salt solution any longer than necessary, so pay attention. Remove the silver from the pan, rinse thoroughly, and dry immediately.

The Tepid-Bath Method

This method cleans your silver just the way the hot-bath method does, but more slowly. Fill a disposable aluminum foil pan, or a plastic bowl lined with aluminum foil, with tepid water. Add about ¼ cup of salt and enough liquid fabric softener (any brand will do) to make the water cloudy.

Add your silver to the bath, making sure that each piece touches the aluminum foil. Let stand for about an hour, depending on how filthy your silver is. Remove the silver promptly, rinse, and dry thoroughly.

The sour-milk method of cleaning a small piece of silver

The Sour-Milk Method

No, you don't have to wait until the milk in your refrigerator sours. Just pour milk into a bowl big enough to hold your silver object. Squeeze the juice of a lemon into the milk. It'll sour the minute the lemon juice hits it.

Put your silver into the bowl, making sure it is completely covered with milk. Allow it to soak for several hours or overnight. Remove, rinse in cold water, and dry immediately.

AND SOME NOT-SO-EASY WAYS

The "I Insist on Working" Method

If you *must* scrub to be happy, here's the recipe for you. First, make sure all items are sterling—do not use this treatment on silver plate.

Use 1 cup of cigar ashes (burn the cigars outside in the backyard, please), 2 tablespoons of baking soda, and enough water to make a paste. Then hold your nose and rub it on the silver. Rinse in cold water and dry immediately.

You can also use tartar-control toothpaste to clean silver, or a paste made of baking soda and water.

Removing Egg Stains

If you've ever served deviled eggs on a silver platter, you know what unsightly stains can result. Remove the stains by rubbing them with salt, then wash the piece in warm soapy water, rinse in cool water, and dry thoroughly. It is important to get all the salt off. Any residue will pit your silver.

Eight Great Ways to Retard Tarnish

You can't completely protect your silver from tarnish, but you can certainly slow down its formation.

- **No Rubber Gloves, Ever!** Never handle your silver with rubber or latex gloves. Contact with rubber will cause your silver to darken. Sometimes it makes me think I have to give up my hands for my silver antiques. At the very least, you can keep your nails from turning black by digging them into a bar of soap before you start cleaning the silver. Be sure to rinse all the soap off the silver.

- **Store Silver Really, Really Clean.** Even the tiniest bit of soap residue will hasten tarnish, so always rinse thoroughly.

- **Dry, Dry Again.** After you polish silver, always dry it thoroughly. Then leave it out for a few hours to be sure it's *completely* dry. If you store silver that's still damp, it can tarnish, rust, or even corrode.

- **Choose Chalk.** Put a piece of white chalk into the drawer or box where you're storing your silver. Be sure it doesn't touch the silver. It will absorb moisture and retard tarnish.

- **The Bag's the Thing.** Don't store silver in ordinary felt bags or on felt drawer liners. Felt gives off hydrogen sulfide (like eggs!) and causes tarnish. Instead, use treated felt

Ordinary chalk will retard tarnish when stored in the same container as silver.

bags or cloth, available at fabric stores. Or try the tarnish-preventive strips sold in housewares stores.

- **Observe the "No Paint" Rule.** Don't store silver objects near latex paint. Not that you'd keep your fine silver tea service in the garage, but I thought you'd want to know. You can't display silver on latex-painted shelves, either. Oak darkens silver, too, so don't display it on oak tables or shelves.

- **No Breathing Allowed.** Like most metals, silver will combine with the oxygen in the air to form tarnish. To create a protective barrier, polish your silver with furniture wax. Do not, however, wax objects in which you are planning to serve food or beverages.

- **Things *Not* to Leave in Silver Containers.** Alcoholic beverages, high-acid foods or beverages (such as tomato sauce or fruit juice), perfume, cosmetics, and salt can all stain or damage silver.

Dos and Don'ts for Storing Silver

- **Do** wrap silver pieces individually in tissue paper and store them in an airtight container.

- **Do** throw a few mothballs in the container, but don't let them come in direct contact with the silver.

- **Do** put an aluminum foil strip in with the silver.

- **Don't** store silver plate in newspaper. Ink can strip off the thin layer of silver.

- **Don't** use rubber bands to secure the wrappings. Remember how rubber gloves darken silver? So do rubber bands.

- **Don't** store silver objects in the attic. Heat can hasten tarnishing.

Repairs

If a handle comes off, say, your family heirloom coffeepot, have a professional resolder it for you. The repair won't devalue the piece much. It will, however, cost a bundle to have it done—approximately fifty percent of the overall value.

If a silver object is dented, don't try to fix the dents yourself. Take it to a professional. Always do this promptly. Dents that are repeatedly polished can turn into holes.

Oh, and one more thing: When you display your stunningly shiny silver, it always looks best against a red background.

Bijou Benefactors

Or, Neat Tricks for

Taking Care of Your

Collectible Jewelry

W e'll never know the answer to this question, but I wonder if Marc Antony would have even noticed Cleopatra's cleavage if there hadn't been a honkin' big piece of jewelry dangling in it. The truth is, Cleo probably didn't look anything like Elizabeth Taylor. From what I hear, she was a scrawny thing who didn't have much cleavage in which to nestle jewels, and she was never going to win the Miss Alexandria Pageant. You also have to wonder whether she was short a couple of hieroglyphics, because she married her twelve-year-old brother.

Okay, so she didn't have looks or brains, but she had great style. Having yourself delivered to the emperor of Rome in a rug takes creativity and also the ability to hold your breath for a long period of time. After all, they didn't have wet-dry vacs in ancient Egypt,

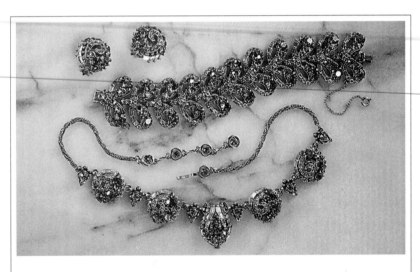

Collectible jewelry is quite delicate and should not be washed with soap and water.

and the inside of those things must have been pretty ripe. Cleopatra was a practical girl as well. When her prepubescent brother-husband drowned, the young widow took up with Julius Caesar, emperor of Rome (and he made a pretty good salad, too!). When she went to Rome to present Caesar with the son he fathered while visiting her in Egypt, he was assassinated. So, she returned home to Egypt to await the arrival of Marc Antony, with whom she had twins. It's amazing how these things work out.

Cleo's life was not without its tribulations, of course. Someone was always trying to kill her or her children, and the citizens of Rome didn't exactly shout "Huzzah!" when she arrived. Also, her relationship with Marc definitely suffered as the result of poor communication. When they were at war against Octavian, she spread a rumor that she had killed herself. I have no idea why; maybe it was the ancient Egyptian idea of a good joke. Antony heard the report and stabbed himself. Boy oh boy, these two were made for each other. When she heard what he had done, she had the last laugh by killing herself with a poisonous snake. Or perhaps she simply decided that, since everyone who married her bit the dust shortly afterward, she should avoid any further contact with men.

Cleo apparently had many fabulous baubles, as befitted the queen of Egypt. She may not have been a beauty or a genius, but she knew how to accessorize. When she hit the local discos with Marc, I'm sure she was very well put together. And I'm willing to bet that her jewelry was immaculately sparkly, no matter how dirty the rugs were. All of it was in good repair, too. But not repaired by her, of course.

Today, we have the means to clean, repair, and maintain our jewelry in queenly fashion. And it can pretty much all be done using the same stuff that was available in Cleopatra's day.

Making Your Jewelry Sparkle

Almost All-Purpose Cleaner

This almost all-purpose cleaner can be used on gold jewelry and costume jewelry with unfoiled rhinestones. Do not use it for pearls, opals, or costume jewelry containing foiled rhinestones. Rhinestones with foiled backs will eventually turn cloudy or black when exposed to moisture.

1. Mix Top Job or Mr. Clean with water, using 1 part cleaner to 2 parts water.

2. Apply the mixture to the jewelry with a soft toothbrush, or use it in an ultrasonic cleaner. If the jewelry has glued-in stones, the ultrasonic cleaner may dissolve the glue and cause the stones to fall out. Empty the ultrasonic cleaner into a strainer to catch any loose stones. You can glue them back into place later; see "Replacing Rhinestones" (page 79).

3. Rinse and dry the jewelry thoroughly.

Bakelite Beautification

You already have plenty of products around the house that are excellent for cleaning Bakelite jewelry. In fact, any cleaner that contains ammonia will work: Dow Bathroom Cleaner, Windex, and Turtle Wax Super Hard Shell car wax are three of the common ones. Of course, there's always plain old ammonia.

Saturate a cotton swab with the cleaner and swab the Bakelite; then rinse and dry thoroughly. Do not, however, rinse Bakelite jewelry that includes rhinestones. Wipe the jewelry with a clean, damp cloth instead, being careful not to wet the stones.

Chain, Chain, Chain

Here are three quick and easy methods for cleaning tarnish from your silver chains:

- **White Vinegar.** Use a mixture of white vinegar and water, applied with a soft toothbrush. Rinse and wipe dry.

- **Hair Shampoo.** Apply hair shampoo (or the vinegar mixture) to a soft cloth or towel. Wrap the cloth around the chain and pull the chain through. Rinse and dry thoroughly.

- **Lemon Juice and Salt.** Sprinkle coarse salt on a damp cloth. Squeeze the juice of a lemon onto the cloth. Pull the chain through, as above. Rinse and dry thoroughly.

Fine Jewelry

Jewelry made with precious metals and gemstones may be cleaned with toothpaste, applied with a toothbrush. Rinse and dry.

CARING FOR COPPER JEWELRY

Removing Tarnish

To clean heavily tarnished copper jewelry that doesn't have any stones or enameling, immerse it in a can of tomatoes overnight. (I don't need to tell you not to eat the tomatoes afterward, do I?) Rinse and dry it thoroughly. To restore the beautiful patina, simply expose the jewelry to the air for a few days.

Damaged Lacquer

Some copper jewelry is lacquered by the maker to prevent tarnish, but lacquer also prevents a high shine. If some of the lacquer has been compromised and your jewelry has black spots, you can remove the rest of the lacquer before cleaning. Apply nail-polish remover or acetone with a cotton swab. Then use the tomato tarnish removal method described above.

If you prefer to leave the lacquer on, and you want to match the color of the exposed spot to the rest of the piece, clean only that spot by applying ketchup with a cotton swab. Then apply heat from the underside, holding the piece over a steaming teakettle, a burner on the stove, or even a light bulb until the spot matches the rest of the piece.

TREATING CORROSION OR "GREEN GUNK"

VERDIGRIS, OR corrosion, is the green gunk that affects costume jewelry exposed to moisture. If not checked, corrosion will spread and can ruin the whole piece. It can even spread to other pieces stored in the same container. There is more than one way to remove it, but the only way to prevent its return is to dry, dry, *dry*.

- **Ketchup.** My favorite way to treat corrosion is with ketchup, because it stays where you put it instead of running all over the place. Use a cotton swab to apply the ketchup to just the corroded area and leave it on for 20 minutes, no longer. Then wipe off the ketchup, rinse thoroughly, and dry with a blow dryer on the coolest setting.

- **Vinegar and Salt.** Add 1 tablespoon of white vinegar and 1 tablespoon of salt to 1 cup of very hot water. Use an old soft toothbrush to apply the solution to the affected area and get it into all the crevices. Rinse in clean water and dry with a blow dryer on the coolest setting.

Even if you think your jewelry is dry, before you put it away, dry it again with a blow dryer on the lowest setting. Store jewelry in an open tray, in a low-humidity environment, with a couple of packets of silica gel thrown into the tray. Never store pieces of jewelry touching each other. Never, ever, store your jewelry in sealed plastic bags.

Protecting Your Pearls

PEARLS ARE tricky. They're affected by things like perfume, hairspray, and makeup. They must be handled carefully.

After you take off your pearls, gently wipe them with a soft cloth. To clean pearls, moisten a very soft cloth with a little olive oil. Gently rub each pearl individually with the cloth.

Real pearls must be cleaned individually and very gently.

Replacing Rhinestones

IT'S A simple enough procedure to replace a missing rhinestone in a piece of costume jewelry, but it requires good lighting and a steady hand. Use a glue that dries clear. Two of my favorites are E6000 and G-S Hypo-Tube cement.

1. Carefully examine the cup that held the rhinestone. If you see any old glue in the cup, dislodge it using a toothpick or a pin. Dental tools are great for this. Your dentist may be willing to give you some old ones, but if not, they're available at some drugstores and many flea markets.

2. Put the stone face up on a table. Roll a piece of wax between your fingers to soften it, and then press it onto the stone to lift it.

3. Squeeze a little glue or cement onto a toothpick or pin, and put it into the cup. (If you're using G-S Hypo-Tube cement, you can squeeze the cement directly into the cup—Hypo-Tube comes with a fine, needlelike applicator.) Count to ten and deposit the stone from the wax into the cup. Use a pin to maneuver the stone and seat it properly in the cup. Wipe away any excess glue immediately. Leave the piece undisturbed for 24 hours.

No More Tangles

To KEEP your chains from getting knotted, store each one in a straw. Open the clasp on the chain. Drop one end of the chain into a plastic or paper drinking straw. Bend the straw around in a circle and close the clasp. It may be necessary to cut the straw to an appropriate length so you don't stretch or break the chain when you close the clasp.

Porcelain

Prescriptives

Or, How to Repair

and Maintain Your

Porcelains and Pottery

M y husband, Artie (He Who Is The Light Of My Life), and his younger brother Don were the children of working parents. I never knew their mother and father, but I think it's safe to say they were as beleaguered as any other two-career couple forced to leave their two normally rambunctious boys at home alone during the day.

In the years I've known HWITLOML and his brother, I've been regaled with many stories of mayhem and mischief. I think I'll spare you, for now, the story of how the blanket got burned, and the one about how every boy in the neighborhood came to be sent outside in the middle of summer wearing winter clothes, and just discuss the tale that's relevant here: The Bowling Pin Fights.

Porcelains and pottery are among the most popular decorative accessories in the collecting world.

These boys get credit for creativity. They amused themselves when they were home alone by invading the living room and taking cover behind various pieces of upholstered furniture (HWITLOML tells me he favored the space behind the sofa). They then performed war maneuvers by hurling plastic bowling pins at each other.

Before you ask, let me say that I am reasonably certain that Don and Artie are of normal intellectual capacity. Now, to go on with the story.

I'm sure you can see the potential for catastrophe here. The boys fully realized this potential by scoring a direct hit to their mother's prized figurine, a chariot pulled by two horses, causing grievous injury to one of the horses in the form of an amputated leg. Naturally, Artie says Don broke the statue and Don claims Artie did it. They both agree, however, that they conspired to prevent their parents from noticing the results of their demolition derby by gluing the leg back onto the horse. Even today, HWITLOML is not very good at the art of reattachment, so I'm not envisioning a high level of aesthetic accomplishment. In fact, both brothers assure me that the result of their feverish repair job "looked pretty crappy."

What mystifies me is that their parents apparently never noticed, or at least never cared to comment on, either the painfully obvious injury or the painfully incompetent veterinary services visited upon the poor horse. To the boys this meant, "Wow, we got away with this! This proves what we've always known: we are *geniuses!*"

Which was not a good thing for the poor horse, because the bowling pin fights continued and the noble steed "got it" again, in the other front leg. He not only "got it" with a plastic bowling pin. He also "got it" with another shot of Duco cement, which formed a yellow line across his leg—a leg that now resided on his body at a frighteningly bizarre angle. I would venture to guess that this little equine must have looked at this point like a Salvador Dalí sculpture.

Still, neither parent noticed the figurine, or else they both pretended not to notice for reasons of their own, which is why Artie and Don are both convinced that they are not only phenomenally clever but that they're both hilariously funny as well.

My job here is to show you ways to repair and care for your own porcelain and pottery *objets* so that, should an unfortunate bowling pin attack ever take place in your home, no one will have to pretend they haven't noticed the victims. All the horses (and everything else) will look good as new.

CLEANING AND STAIN REMOVAL

PORCELAINS SHOULD only be washed by hand, never in the dishwasher. Put a towel in the bottom of your sink as a cushion to prevent breakage. Use only tepid water and mild soap. Avoid very hot water, as sudden temperature changes could cause the porcelain to crack.

Here are a few unusual but effective cleaning agents:

- **Cream of Tartar.** Coffee, tea, and other minor stains can be removed from porcelain by rubbing cream of tartar on the spot with a wet cloth. Rinse in tepid water.

- **Hydrogen Peroxide.** Hydrogen peroxide works wonders on rust or other stubborn stains that won't yield to cream of tartar. Buy the 30 percent–strength peroxide sold in beauty-supply stores. Place your porcelain item in a bowl or basin. Add ¼ cup of peroxide to 2 cups of water. To this solution, add 4 drops of ammonia. Wear gloves to protect your hands. Pour enough of the solution in to cover the stain. Let sit for 5 minutes; then rinse very thoroughly and dry. Repeat if necessary.

To protect fine porcelains from breakage, wash by hand, and line the sink with a towel.

- **Coca-Cola.** For stubborn stains on vitreous china, or porcelain with a high silica content (the stuff that, when you look at it, you can never decide whether it's porcelain or glass), put the item in a bowl or basin, and pour in enough Coca-Cola to cover the stain. Let it sit for an hour. Rinse thoroughly.

- **Tang.** Tang orange breakfast drink also works well. Mix it full strength, pour it into a stained porcelain bowl or cup, and allow to stand for a few hours.

Repairing Hurt Porcelains and Pottery

You can repair chips, cracks, and even breaks in porcelain and pottery in a few simple steps.

Chips

1. Use wood filler (made of wood fiber and sawdust) to fill the chip, smoothing and shaping it with your finger.

2. When the filler is dry, use an emery board to sand it smooth and even with the surrounding surface.

This porcelain has been invisibly repaired with items found around the house.

3. Color with paint pens to match the surrounding area. Paint pens are available at art- and-craft supply stores.

Hairline Cracks

Use this method only on hairline cracks in the thinnest eggshell porcelains.

1. Fill a pot with milk. Immerse the porcelain in the milk, making sure the crack is submerged.

2. Bring the milk to a boil. Then lower the heat and simmer gently for half an hour or so. The protein in the milk will fuse the crack.

Breaks

Clean breaks, with no missing parts, can be glued back together. Where most people go wrong is in choosing the glue. You want something that won't turn brown and show. My favorite glue for mending pottery and porcelain is clear E6000.

1. Be sure both halves of the item are clean. Apply glue to both pieces. Wait a few moments for the glue to get tacky.

2. Press the halves together, and tape them or hold snugly with a rubber band. Remove any visible excess glue immediately.

3. Wait at least 24 hours before you take off the tape or rubber band.

4. If the break was not clean and there's a small space along the mend, follow the instructions for mending chips (page 85).

Fixing a Leaky Vessel

Got a leaky vase? Coat the inside with a thick layer of paraffin wax, and it'll hold water without leaking.

Safe Storage

Don't stack porcelains. Store flat pieces, like dishes, with foam sheets between them. Otherwise, cushion porcelains with materials like bubble wrap, foam rubber, towels, or felt.

To safely store porcelains, use bubble wrap between plates and around three-dimensional objects.

Pottery Pointers

- **Keep It Clean.** Before washing pottery, place a towel in the bottom of the sink for safety. Use warm water and mild dishwashing soap.

- **Stain Removal.** For stains on pottery, add bleach to the wash water and clean with a soft cloth.

- **Stubborn Stain Removal.** It may be necessary to let the pottery soak in bleach and soapy water for a while. If the stains still don't come out, rinse and repeat until they do.

- **White Ironstone.** Stains on the inside of white ironstone can be removed by filling the object with a 40-percent peroxide and 60-percent water solution and allowing it to sit for two to four weeks. Then line the bottom of your oven with aluminum foil, preheat to 250°F, and put the ironstone in the oven for 20 minutes. Take the ironstone out of the oven, allow to cool, and wash in soapy water.

Saving the
Music

Or, Recommendations for
Radios, Record Players,
and Records

Nowadays, youngsters who are shopping for music are likely to say, "Records? What are those?"

But if you were born before 1980 or so, you're bound to remember those flat discs, shiny and most often black, that you could plop down on a piece of equipment no longer present in most homes. After putting the disc in place and pressing a button, you could watch a plastic arm descend on the disc, stopping just before it made contact. Mounted on the end of the plastic arm was a sharp little metal device called a *needle*. When the needle landed on the disc, lo and behold, music came out of your speakers. Of course, it wasn't music of the quality you'd expect from a Walkman, but it was music, nonetheless.

When I was a child, even though tape players had been invented, what we had in our house was a record player. In fact, we kids had our *own* record player. No one said my folks were stupid. I'm sure their big high-fidelity system lived a longer and healthier life because we weren't allowed to use it.

We also had individual musical tastes. When I look back on it, I just have to shake my head. Of course, I feel the same way when I look back on some of my ex-boyfriends. What *was* I thinking?

One year I requested, as a gift from my parents, a

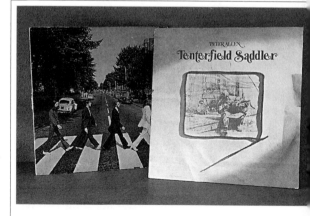

Record albums, once the world's most popular form of recorded music, are no longer mass produced.

recording of Eddie Fisher singing "Oh, My Papa." I have no idea what possessed them to actually give it to me. I played it at least a thousand times a day. I can't recall what happened to that record, but I'll bet my father smashed it to smithereens while I was out playing in the yard one day, which is exactly what I would have done if I were Dad. It must have driven everyone in the house insane. Of course, when I think of Eddie Fisher today, I also think, "Eeeeuuuuuwww!"

My brother Arnie's favorite record was, for about a year, the theme song from the TV show *Zorro*. After that, it was the theme song from *Davy Crockett*. I know who smashed those two records, but I'm not telling.

I don't remember my sister Evelyn's favorite record. I do remember that we used to attend, occasionally, a meeting of Grandpa and Grandma's group, the Poloner Society. This was a family circle mutual-benefit-type society, and the meetings were always held in Manhattan at some rental hall. Cold-cut platters were always served and there was always a waiter whose job it was to carve sandwich meats to order. It was at one of these meetings that I had what amounted to a culinary epiphany.

Grandma said, "Come, *Judele*, I'll take you to get a *sennevich*."

No problem there. I was ready for a sandwich. We went up to the carving table where the white-coated waiter was expertly carving this enormous curved piece of meat. Grandma said, "You want some tongue?"

"Grandma," I asked, eyeing the big slab of flesh with apprehension, "when you have a tongue sandwich, are you eating the actual cow's tongue?"

"Of course!" Grandma answered. "Vudden?"

And so began the march toward vegetarianism.

Entertainment was always a part of these enormous extended family gatherings. But it was the children who were expected to provide it. You had to sing a song, recite a poem, dance a jig, do something. This, of course, was never a problem for the three Katz children. The problem arose when you wanted us to shut up and sit down. On this particular day, having finished my lovely plate of coleslaw, potato salad, and lettuce and tomatoes with rye bread and mustard, I chose to sing "Rock n' Roll Waltz," something I'd apparently heard on the radio that week. Arnie sang "Oh, My Papa." I don't know which is more amazing: the fact that he could possibly want to sing—much less hear—that song ever again, or the fact that my parents didn't clap their hands over his mouth the minute he uttered the first note.

Evelyn decided on a song we'd all been taught as babies. It was sung to the tune of "Ach Du Lieber Augustine," an old German song, but this version had Yiddish lyrics. The words went:

Oy, de Bubba cucht luckshen, cucht luckshen, cucht luckshen.
Oy, de Bubba cucht luckshen.
Zup, Zaydeh, zup.

In English, the words are:

Oh, the Grandma is cooking noodles, cooking noodles, cooking noodles.
Oh, the Grandma is cooking noodles.
Soup, Grandpa, soup!

Which is a very nice, simple song.

However, when Evelyn, who was five at the time, got up to sing, the entire audience dissolved into hysterics. Grown men were falling off their chairs. Grandma laughed so hard she got all red in the face, and Grandpa kept banging the table as tears rolled down his face. All because of one vowel.

Evelyn was singing:

Oy, de Bubba cocht luckshen, cocht luckshen, cocht luckshen . . .

which translated into English means "Oh, the Grandma is performing a bodily function that is resulting in a large pile of noodles on the kitchen floor underneath Grandma . . . Soup, Grandpa, soup!"

The image was, apparently, too much for some people. They were beside themselves with mirth. Great-aunt Anna actually wet her pants. When she announced this to the room in general, there resulted a fresh outburst of uncontrollable laughter. It was at least half an hour before the room was quiet and people were breathing normally again. Evelyn was a star!

Once we got to be teenagers, we were far more obsessed with the radio than with records. There was a rock 'n' roll station in New York called WMCA. The disc jockeys called themselves the WMCA Good Guys. They played the same Top 40 songs over and over and over again, twenty-four hours a day. Isn't it amazing how young people seem comfortable with endless repetition? On Wednesdays, the playlist changed and we were treated to a slightly different roster of Top 40 selections, as old songs were edged off the charts by new ones. We knew every song by heart and, I'm willing to bet, so did our long-suffering parents.

I can remember one summer when WINS, a competing rock 'n' roll station, ran a contest. The station was going to award a cash prize for the best "WINSburn." You were supposed to cut out the station's call letters from pieces of paper and place them somewhere on your body. Then you were supposed to go out into the sun and get a sunburn that showed up the letters. Beaches, rooftops, and front yards all over the metropolitan New York area were filled with young people covered with bits of paper, lying in the sun. And some of this paper was attached to some pretty unusual body parts.

Nowadays, people who collect radios or old vinyl records have an appreciation for rock 'n' roll and for folk music, but I'm quite sure that music about grandmothers with strangely functioning large intestines and questionable dinner menus is not high up there on the topical list. And I'm equally sure that people who collect radios are not allowing their lives to be dictated by them—unless you count getting up at 4 A.M. to get to that tag sale because there was a Bakelite Fada advertised in the newspaper.

TLC FOR YOUR RECORDS

ONCE THEY are scratched, warped, or otherwise damaged, records cannot be restored. It's essential both to buy and maintain them in excellent condition. Here are some keys to caring for them properly.

- **No Stacking Your Platters.** Never store records in a stack. Eventually they will warp or scratch each other. Records should always be stored on edge in their original sleeves.

- **Environmental Control.** Never store records near heat or in high humidity. They will warp like crazy.

- **Dust-free.** Records must be dusted frequently with a soft, lint-free cloth, unless, of course, the records are still sealed in their original shrink-wrap.

- **Labels and Covers.** The condition of the label, picture sleeve, and album cover are very important to maintaining value. If your record has a label that's coming loose, carefully glue it down. If the picture sleeve is wrinkled, press it using the middle setting of your iron, from the wrong side. A cover torn at the seam may be repaired from the inside, with tape. Price stickers can be removed by saturating the tag with lighter fluid (not butane), counting 5 seconds, and then gently peeling off the label. Repeated applications may be needed.

Records in mint condition or, at least, very good condition are the only ones of any monetary value. To check the condition of a record you're not sure about, play it. If you hear cracks and pops, it's scratched and its value is minimal.

RADIOS AND RECORD PLAYERS

RESIST THE urge to restore a wood radio cabinet to a state of perfection. This will actually decrease its value. A vintage wood radio cabinet should have some wear and should look as if it has been used, but not abused. Bakelite, on the other hand, can and should be restored to its former brilliance.

Cleaning and Polishing

Take the radio apart, as far as you can. Some radios are held together with a series of clips. At the very least, the speaker grille is usually detachable. After taking the radio apart, attend to the knobs and trim.

- **Bakelite Parts.** Place Bakelite parts into a sink full of tepid (not hot) water and clean with dishwashing soap. It is important not to use hot water, which may make the plastic brittle. Scrub with a toothbrush, rinse, and dry. Then give the Bakelite parts a coat of paste wax to protect them.

- **Brass Parts.** Brass parts can be cleaned with lemon juice and salt, with vinegar, or with toothpaste, as described in "Brass Beauty" (page 56). If the brass parts were lacquered and the lacquer is now pitted (it almost always will be), remove it with nail-polish remover or acetone. Once the brass is clean and shiny, protect it with a coat of paste wax.

- **Chrome Parts.** Clean chrome parts with rubbing alcohol followed by a coat of paste wax.

- **Bakelite Cabinet.** Use tepid water and dishwashing soap to remove the surface dirt. A commercial polish called Simichrome works well for polishing Bakelite, but any household cleaner containing ammonia will work well, too. Coat with paste wax after the Bakelite has thoroughly air-dried.

- **Wood Cabinet.** Clean a dirty wood cabinet with waterless hand cleaner. Remember, you don't want it to be immaculate.

Making Minor Repairs

- **Replacing Missing Knobs.** The cap from a 2-liter Coca-Cola bottle makes a great substitute for a missing knob. Fill the cap with plaster or spackling compound. When dry, spray-paint the piece satin black, drill a hole, and screw your new knob onto the cabinet. You'll have to change all the knobs on the radio to match. Half-gallon milk bottle caps, prepared in the same manner, are a good substitute for larger knobs.

- **Mending Cracks in Bakelite.** To repair clean breaks in a Bakelite radio, you can use Super Glue (cyanoacrylate). Put some Super Glue on a pin or needle. Apply from the back side of the Bakelite, sparingly, just so the glue runs into the crack. After it dries, use a single-edged razor blade to shave off any excess glue.

- **Mending Deep Cracks.** For cracks that gape, try this method: Use a file to wear down the Bakelite in an inconspicuous spot, such as the back of a knob or the inside of the cabinet. Mix your filings with clear-drying glue, such as E6000, and use the mixture to fill the gaps. This has the advantage of being a perfect color match.

- **Mending Scratches.** Improve the appearance of badly scratched Bakelite with an emery board or fine sandpaper. Carefully sand out the scratches, then polish with paste wax.

- **Restoring Original Color.** Bakelite undergoes color changes over the years. If it is important to you that the radio be its original color, you can sand it to reveal that original hue. Be *very careful*—you don't want to end up with an uneven surface.

- **Mending Wood Cabinets.** The most common problem encountered with wooden cabinets is that they come apart at the seams. You can reglue them using a good wood glue. Hold the pieces together with clamps until the glue dries. If you are regluing more than one side of a cabinet, you'll need to check that each side is square before proceeding. Check the first side with a T-square before you reglue the second, and so forth.

- **Doctoring Dents.** To repair small dents in wood, hold the dented part over a boiling teakettle. The steam should cause the dented area to swell.

When it comes to refurbishing the inside of your radio, unless you're a gearhead like HWITLOML, leave it to the professionals.

Terrific
Textiles

Or, Restoring the

Original Splendor of Your

Vintage Linens, Silks, and Rugs

Thereʼs probably no more tactile connection between the generations than the comfort of a wonderful old textile. Think of your old camp blanket, your great-grandmotherʼs quilt, the beautiful beaded twenties flapper dress you found at a vintage clothing shop. The softness, the warmth, the cool, the smooth, the rough—all are part of the memories.

Vintage clothing requires careful maintenance and storage.

Handing down linens and blankets from hope chest to hope chest is a beloved tradition for families everywhere. Many brides choose to wear the wedding gowns their mothers and grandmothers wore.

The difficulty for collectors of vintage textiles is that so many of them were not meant for display alone. They got used. They suffer, sometimes, from the process of living. That beautiful nineteenth-century crazy quilt may bear the scars of the thousand or more nights spent beneath a child who climbed into Mama and Papa's bed, milk bottle in tow, for protection from the trolls under the cot in the nursery.

Your sensational Edwardian gown may have been through one too many formal dinners, including a few with too much chocolate sauce on the menu. Old textiles tend to keep secrets, too, hiding food and other stains for years, then giving them up when you least expect it. So if you're going to collect vintage textiles, it's important to know how to ensure they'll be beautiful for a long time to come.

My extended family tree included a branch in which all brides wore the Family Wedding Gown, a slinky 1930s affair with an Art Deco headpiece. The gown, as I remember it, was made of ivory silk and was one of those elegant floor-length numbers with a long train suspended from the neckline, like a royal cape. The matriarch of the family, the grandmother, originally wore it. After that, it had served as a bridal gown for each of the grandmother's three daughters, then each of their daughters. Finally (and I do mean finally), my third cousin Sara became engaged and had the gown brought up from the basement closet so she could try it on.

It so happened that the gown was a perfect fit. That, I think, is the beginning of where things went horribly wrong. If it had needed alterations, the seamstress would surely have pointed out that the gown had been improperly stored. Silk doesn't take well to improper storage.

The wedding day arrived. Hundreds of relatives and friends descended on the chapel for the ceremony and ensuing festival of extreme overeating. The organ began to play, as the bridesmaids and groomsmen made their way down the white carpet and under the canopy. Finally, the bride advanced down the aisle, flanked by her mother and her father.

Jewish custom dictates that the bride and her parents stop about halfway down the aisle, where her mother kisses her goodbye. The bridegroom, who has been standing at the altar watching his beloved approach, then comes down the aisle to meet her. Her father lifts her veil, kisses her good-bye, and she travels the rest of the way to the altar on the arm of her husband-to-be.

In the case of Cousin Sara's wedding, all the walking and kissing took place rather smoothly, except for one thing. When the father of the bride kissed his daughter and sent her off, he happened to be standing on her train. As she walked down the aisle on the arm of her intended, the train—and the back half of her dress along with it—remained in the aisle with her parents. Sara arrived at the altar in the front of her dress, and her slip, of course, while the back of her dress languidly stretched itself out on the carpet in the middle of the chapel.

For a moment, dead silence fell over the room. The guests had absolutely no idea how to react to the situation, not having consulted Miss Manners' chapter on wedding etiquette for events where the bride is apparently stuck in a Charlie Chaplin movie. After about ten seconds, a giggle or two escaped, followed by a chorus of "shushes." There were quite a few "Oy veys!" Then, suddenly, there was an avalanche of conversation, as everyone loudly recounted a formal affair he or she had attended where there was some embarrassing occurrence.

The bride's attendants had gathered around her to obstruct the view of her lacy underthings, while her female relatives ran to the bridal room to find a robe for her. All this activity was unnecessary, since nobody was currently paying the slightest attention to what was going on under the canopy.

The noise swelled, the ceremony forgotten, as the tales became more and more bizarre. My favorite was the story about my aunt's aunt, who sat up at her own funeral, had a look around, and waved to her daughter in the front row. Without recounting the whole creepy story, let me just say that a convoy of ambulances was required to take all the fainting victims to the hospital where, once revived, they took turns telling the old lady it was just a dream. But I digress.

Rest assured, Sara got married that night and, if you saw her wedding album, you'd never even know there'd been a problem. All the formal photos had been taken before the ceremony, when she was still fully clothed. Everything after the ceremony was pho-tographed, amid much mirth, from the front. A good time was had by all.

The point of all this is that Sara's wedding could have been a memorable event because it was so beautiful, instead of being memorable because it was so like a Three Stooges finale. If only her family had known how to take care of her beautiful old wedding gown, it could have gone on to appear at Sara's daughter's wedding. Needless to say, the gown was permanently retired—what was left of it, that is.

LOVELY LINENS

Follow the Basics

Fresh stains and dirt are much easier to remove from textiles than old ones. Do it sooner, and you'll be glad later. After using soap or any other substance to treat fabric or remove stains, rinse thoroughly, *removing all traces of the product used*.

And be patient. Patience is the single most important requirement for working with antique textiles. Be prepared to repeat cleaning steps over and over, until your treasure is spotless.

Protecting Textiles

- **Moths!** These critters love natural fibers like wool. They must be killed. When you first purchase a vintage textile, shake it off outside. If you see any eggs shake out, or if you have any other reason to suspect the presence of moth eggs, put the item in a plastic bag, seal it completely, and place it in your freezer for a few days. Freezing kills the eggs.

- **For All Washable Fabrics.** Use a Neutrogena bar in the Original Formula. This mild, nonabrasive soap is safe for old washable fabrics and is widely available. Cut the 3.5-ounce bar into 8 pieces. Use one piece for every ½ gallon of washing water. Dissolve each piece in a cup of water before adding it to the washing water.

- **Think Gentle.** Wet fabric is weakened fabric. Don't wash any vintage textile if there is something gentler you can do, such as brushing or vacuuming. Never hang soaking-wet fabric. Roll the item in white towels first to remove excess moisture. Lay fragile fabrics out flat to dry.

- **Whiten and Brighten.** To treat general yellowing and to help remove stains of unknown origin, soak old textiles in cold water in which you have dissolved a denture-cleaning tablet. Rinse thoroughly.

- **Test First.** No matter what cleaning or stain-removal method you plan to use, always test it in an inconspicuous place first.

- **Display without Damage.** Lengthy exposure to direct sunlight is the worst thing that can happen to an old textile. Display your textiles in a shaded environment.

Laundering Tips

- **Soak Fine Cottons and Linens.** Soak your fine-textured cottons and linens in distilled water with a mild soap or detergent—no perfumes or additives allowed. Some clear dishwashing liquids are good. A long soaking can work wonders, and it is safe, even if done for days. Lay items flat to dry.

- **Render Linens Spotless.** Add ¼ cup Cascade dishwashing detergent and ½ cup Clorox chlorine bleach to 1 gallon of *cold* water. Soak the items in this solution for at least 2 hours. Then launder as usual. They'll be spotless!

- **Eliminate Yellowing.** To prevent and eliminate yellowing, soak sturdy fabrics for long periods, even for days, in a mild chlorine bleach solution (1 teaspoon bleach to 1 cup water). Rinse thoroughly, always in cold water. Add a small amount of white vinegar to the last rinse to get the last vestiges of bleach out of the fibers. Hang items in the sun to dry.

- **Banish Wrinkles.** Are your linens coming out of the washing machine all wrinkled? You may be overcrowding them. Overloaded washing machines result in linens that don't come clean and are excessively wrinkled.

- **Rinse Away.** To extend the life of your cottons and linens, always rinse them thoroughly after washing. Hard water leaves mineral deposits in the fibers, eventually causing damage. If you live in a hard-water area, always do the final rinse in distilled water.

- **Savor the Sun.** Dry your linens on a clothesline in the sunshine. It will make them look bright, smell fresh, and feel crisp.

Treating Red Wine Stains

Are your best tablecloths languishing in a closet because you're afraid of wine stains? Follow these steps for removing red wine stains and your fine linens will be out on the table in no time.

1. Saturate the stain with tepid water and cover with a layer of table salt. Rub the salt in and allow it to sit for 5 minutes (longer if the stain isn't fresh).

2. Stretch the fabric across the top of a large bowl and secure with a rubber band. Put the bowl in the sink.

3. Boil water in a teakettle. Lift the kettle about 3 feet above the bowl and carefully pour the boiling water on the stain.

4. Rinse thoroughly and launder the tablecloth as usual.

Removing Rust and Other Stubborn Marks

Try this method to remove rust, brown or yellow marks, dust marks, and other stains that appear to have been left in the fabric a long time.

1. Squeeze the juice from lemons onto the stain, then sprinkle with table salt.

2. Put the item in bright sunlight for a few hours.

3. Wash with mild soap or detergent.

   Repeat steps 1 through 3 as necessary.

Treating Lipstick and Other Greasy Stains

Use any oil-free eye-makeup remover to tackle lipstick or other greasy stains on natural fibers.

Put the eye-makeup remover on a clean cloth and blot the stain over and over again, changing cloths frequently. If this doesn't work, stretch the fabric out on a clean towel and pour the remover directly onto the stain. Let it sit for 20 minutes, then blot. Rinse thoroughly with cold water.

VINTAGE LACE

THE WOMEN'S movement is partly responsible for the upsurge of interest in vintage textiles. Most were, of course, made by women. There's no more elaborate evidence of a woman's handiwork than a piece of fine lace.

Here are some tips to help preserve or restore your vintage lace:

- **Baste First.** To prevent fine lace from falling apart during cleaning, baste it to a sturdier fabric. Make sure the support fabric is made of cotton or another natural fiber and is either white or free of dyes. Unbleached muslin is a good choice.

- **Remove the Tarnish.** Lace made of gold or silver threads may eventually turn black. To remove tarnish, use an old toothbrush dipped in white wine to clean the lace.

- **Press It.** Lace ribbons can be safely pressed by drawing them across a warm light bulb.

SENSATIONAL SILKS

YES, SILK is washable, but you must be careful about dyes. Test an inconspicuous place, like a seam allowance, first.

My favorite cleaner for getting stains out of silks is hydrogen peroxide. I use it straight from the bottle on stains, and I also soak silks in a solution of ½ cup peroxide to ½ gallon of cold water. Soak for at least an hour, longer if the stain is stubborn. Then rinse thoroughly in cold water, adding white vinegar to the last rinse. Squeeze gently—*don't* twist or wring—and lay flat to dry.

Vintage Clothing

Nowadays, every fashionable wardrobe includes at least one or two pieces of vintage clothing. Vintage pieces mix so well with contemporary ensembles, and they are usually much better values than comparable new items. But vintage clothing is different: it's been previously worn. This means it may need some help from you before it's wearable again.

- **Perspiration Stains.** Ever buy a lovely article of vintage clothing, only to find that the underarm area has perspiration stains? As long as the article is washable, soak it in a solution of 1 part ammonia to 2 parts water for 30 minutes. Then rinse and hang to dry. Or, try a strong solution of white vinegar and water (the same strength 1:2). Both mixtures work amazingly well.

- **Rust Stains.** If your gorgeous Victorian or Edwardian whites have rust stains, squeeze lemon juice on the stain and lay the clothes in the bright morning sunlight. By afternoon, the stains will be gone. You can try fresh lemon juice on colored clothing, too, but test first in an inconspicuous place.

- **Multipurpose Stain Remover.** Hydrogen peroxide works wonders on a variety of stains. It's especially useful with vintage clothing, where you may have no way to identify the source of the stain. Buy 30-percent-strength peroxide, sold in beauty-supply stores. Add ¼ cup of peroxide to 2 cups of water. To this solution, add 4 drops of ammonia. Wear gloves to protect your hands. Wet a cloth with tap water and dampen the stain.

Then dip the cloth into the solution and apply it to the stain. Let sit for 5 minutes. Rinse thoroughly and dry. Repeat if necessary, always wetting the cloth and the stain with water before applying the peroxide solution.

RUGS AND CARPETS

Refurbishing Tips

- **Vibrant Color.** To brighten the color in a rug, mix 1 cup of white vinegar in 1 gallon of cold water. Dip a broom into this solution and brush the rug with it. No rinsing is necessary.

- **Potato Magic.** To clean rugs and carpets, rub gently with grated raw potato. Rinse by blotting with a clean wet sponge, followed by blotting with dry paper towels.

- **Banish Odors.** To get rid of smells, sprinkle a *dry* rug or carpet with baking soda. Allow to sit for 15 minutes. Vacuum. For stubborn odors, leave the baking soda on overnight. Be sure to test your carpet in an inconspicuous spot for colorfastness first.

- **Wear Repair.** If your antique carpet has a worn spot, you can conceal it. Turn it over, and color the backing with crayon, paint pens, or colored ink to match the carpet pattern.

- **Cigarette Burns.** Carefully cut away the charred fibers with manicure scissors. Or sand the burned area with sandpaper until the damaged fibers are gone.

Treating Stains

The key to getting stains out of carpets and rugs is to tackle the stain as quickly as possible and blot—*never scrub*—with paper towels until you can't get any more of the stain off. If that doesn't do the trick entirely—or if you need to treat stains that have already set—here are some winning methods.

- **Oily Stains.** Cover the stain with flour. Leave it on for 24 hours. Brush off the flour, then brush the rug to bring up the nap. Keep repeating with fresh flour until the stain is gone.

- **Grease.** Wet a bar of Lava soap and rub it on the stain. Rinse well by blotting repeatedly with a clean, wet sponge followed by clean paper towels. If you don't remove all the soap, the area will dry a shade lighter than the rest of the carpet.

- **Chewing Gum.** Rub an ice cube on the gum until it freezes. Use a butter knife or the dull edge of any knife to scrape it off. If any gum is still stuck to the rug, squirt a bit of lighter fluid (not butane) on it and remove the remainder. As soon as the lighter fluid evaporates, rinse the area with soapy water made with dishwashing liquid, followed by a clean wet sponge and blotting with clean paper towels. Use a blow dryer on the coolest setting to dry the rug.

- **Acidic Food Stains.** Shaving cream works well to remove fruit juice or other acid-based food spills, such as tomato sauce or wine sauce. Use just a *tiny bit* of shaving cream, or you'll be rinsing forever. Apply just enough to cover the stain, leaving it on for a few minutes. You may need to repeat this process several times. Blot with a clean wet sponge.

- **Ballpoint-Pen Ink.** Cover the inked area with table salt. Allow it to sit for a few minutes, and then vacuum. Repeat as many times as necessary. Or try this method: Soak a clean rag in milk, squeeze out the excess, and blot the rag on the inky area. Then brush the milk on the surface with a clean toothbrush. Rinse thoroughly, using a clean wet sponge and blotting with clean paper towels. Be sure to get all the milk out, or you'll be dealing with a milk stain.

- **Blood.** Make a paste of equal parts meat tenderizer and cold water. Apply to the stain and leave on for half an hour. Then sponge off with cold water and blot with paper towels. Here's another method: Sprinkle salt on the stain, sprinkle cold water on the salt, and allow enough time for the salt to absorb the blood. Then wipe up the salt mixture with a clean sponge. Blot with clean paper towels.

SIMPLE FABRIC REPAIRS

- **Scorch Marks.** For textiles scorched by an iron, rub the affected area with the cut side of half an onion. Soak the item in cold water for at least one hour; then wash, rinse, and press.

- **Cigarette Burns.** Prevent a burn hole in fabric from getting bigger by hand-stitching around the outside of the hole. Then cross-stitch across the hole to close it up.

STORING YOUR TEXTILES

THE ONE essential step you must take to preserve your treasured textiles is to store them properly (remember Cousin Sara's wedding gown?). Garments that have been worn should be freshly cleaned before storing, even if they're not obviously soiled. And all textiles, including those that have just arrived back from the cleaners, must be examined carefully in bright sunlight. Look for dirt, stains, and wrinkles, and treat them *now*. They may be impossible to remove at a later date.

Never store textiles in plastic bags or boxes. Yes, I know, those plastic bags in which the dry cleaner puts your cleaned garments make storage so convenient. It's so easy to leave the dress on the hanger, in the bag, and store it that way. And it's also easy to slip your antique quilt into the zippered plastic bag your comforter came in. But long-term storage in plastic will destroy your vintage textiles. They should never be kept in plastic wrap, bags, or boxes.

Here's how to safely pack textiles for storage:

- Use only acid-free materials. Box storage is the safest for vintage textiles. Pack items in white tissue paper, being sure to cushion all the folds with tissue. Freshly washed and thoroughly rinsed white cotton sheets may also be used to line boxes, but they must be removed, laundered, and thoroughly rinsed every year or two to prevent acid buildup.

- Put crumpled tissue in the sleeves, shoulders, and bodices of garments. If possible, remove anything made of metal, rubber, or foam, as these can cause stains. If it's not possible to remove these materials, pad them with tissue to prevent them from touching the fabric.

- Do *not* seal boxes. Make slits in them to allow air circulation.

- Store in a cool, dry area where there are no drastic temperature changes. In general, this means that basements, attics, and closets with exterior walls are not acceptable.

- Roll small textiles on cardboard tubes for storage. The tubes must be acid-free and covered with clean white sheeting. Roll the item gently, without tension, avoiding puckers and wrinkles. If the item is fragile or has dye that might run, interleave acid-free tissue as you roll. Wrap

Roll small textiles and quilts onto cardboard tubes for storage.

the whole tube in cotton sheeting and tie loosely with cotton twill tape.

- To prevent moth infestation, place some big sachets in closets and drawers with vintage textiles. Use cotton handkerchiefs or squares of cotton cloth to enclose sprigs of lavender mixed with cedar shavings, fresh citrus peels, and whole cloves. Bring the handkerchief or cloth up around the herbs, gather, and tie with a piece of ribbon or twine. Change the sachets every 6 months.

RECYCLING TEXTILES

WHEN ALL else fails and you can't salvage your precious antique textile intact, you can still make it a part of your life.

- **Tea Dyeing.** If the stains in a vintage white textile just won't come out, dye the cloth ivory or beige by dipping it in weak tepid tea or coffee. Rinse thoroughly.

- **Make a Quilt.** If part of an item is damaged beyond repair but some of the fabric is still sturdy, use the good part in a patchwork quilt.

- **Make Rug Pillows.** Pillows made from pieces of Oriental carpet command very high prices.

- **Save the Down.** You can even recycle the down from an old comforter! Put a brand-new bag in your vacuum cleaner. Open the seams in the comforter, one at a time. As you open each seam, vacuum up the down; you may have to change bags several times to get all the down. Store it right in the vacuum-cleaner bags until you're ready to recycle it.

Last
but Not Least

Or, Tips for Restoring

and Protecting a

Medley of Collectibles

This is the section where I've stuck all those miscellaneous tips and tricks that don't fit into the other categories. In the world of collecting, we frequently find it difficult to categorize everything efficiently. This often results in items with tenuous connections being grouped together in the market. It's why you see toys at paper shows and jewelry at vintage-clothing shows. It's the reason photos show up in the booths of militaria dealers and pinup calendars appear at sports-collectibles shows. Which brings us to the question of what, exactly, qualifies as a sport.

Traditionally, sports are guy things. As an outsider in that realm, I find that many sports make no sense to me. Like, why is boxing considered a sport? I may not be the shiniest penny in the till, but when I see two guys in their undershorts punching each other's lights out, the objective being for one of them to hit the other so hard that he falls unconscious to the floor, I usually think that the bartender should have cut them off about five drinks ago, because that's some pretty unsportsman-like behavior. So why, if this behavior takes place in a ring, is it considered noble?

Miscellaneous collectibles, all of which will benefit from careful cleaning and maintenance.

And how can hunting possibly be considered a sport? There's no competition in it. I say we give the deer a case of beer, a really dumb-looking hat, an orange vest, and an AK-47. Now we have a sport! As questionable as some sports may seem, there is an awful lot of memorabilia attached to them, and it's purchased by both sexes. Go figure.

Music memorabilia is another hot area, one that spans the generations, the genders, and socioeconomic strata. That's because there's such a huge variety of material available, not because there's universal agreement on what is good music.

Sometime during the 1970s, people started showing up on the street, on buses, and in public places carrying giant radios ("boom box" is an apt name). "Music" blared from these boxes, most of it universally hated by everyone who was forced to share it in the street, on subways, or in their own kitchens when the windows were open. Those radios kept getting bigger and bigger, so that their owners had to struggle to carry them around all day. I often thought that smart retailers should have sold them packaged with a color-coordinated hand truck.

Struggle the radio owners did, blasting the rest of us with whatever they wanted to hear. Those who were too bright or too affluent to drag themselves around the street carrying a 50-pound radio cruised the avenues in cars with the windows rolled down, the hatchbacks open, and radios turned up as loud as they could go. At the height of this cacophony, I found myself standing on a corner screaming, "Could you make that a little louder, please? I don't think they can hear you in Armenia!"

Suddenly, fortune smiled on those of us with good taste and a bad headache. The Walkman was invented. At last, peace and quiet prevailed. Or so we thought. The other day, as I hurried down Third Avenue, I could hear someone mumbling incoherently behind me. Having lived in New York City all my life, and having seen everything one can imagine (and some things one could never imagine), I assumed some poor schizophrenic was strolling up the street, conversing with the voices in his head. The occasional recognizable word got out: " . . . the president . . . an incident . . . we are the electorate . . ."

As the voice got louder and closer, I turned around. Approaching me was one of those young people whose trousers are held up solely by the grace of God. He had a CD player in his hand, headphones on his ears, and was apparently attempting to rap along with whatever he was hearing, the lyrics of which he hadn't quite mastered. There is, apparently, no escape from bad music in New York City.

The plus side of this divergence in musical taste is that it has proven useful in the field of crime reduction. Both Australian and Californian authorities report that they've all but eliminated teen drug dealing and violent crimes by youth gangs in certain public places such as bus shelters and shopping centers, simply by playing classical music or pop standards, like Frank Sinatra tunes, nonstop through the loudspeaker systems. What youngster would want to hang around and listen to *that* all day?

Some of my own favorite collectibles are antique kitchen utensils, probably because I used to be a chef. Spending time with restaurant employees can provide you with quite an education. Here are some things that restaurant people know to be fact. I can't explain these things; they're just *true*.

If a pipe smoker comes into the joint, there's going to be a fight. Oh yes, I've seen it a million times. Sometimes it's because the pipe smoker is a creepy guy and all the other testosterone-charged males in the place just want to sock him one in the moosh. Other times, the fight has nothing to do with him. Pay attention next time you're sitting in the local pub or casual eatery.

If the first customer of the evening is off-the-wall, there's a full moon in the sky. Once, my cousin Martin and I were eating in a seafood restaurant in midtown Manhattan. Martin has a goofy and very quick wit. The waiter, a Thai gentleman, was attempting to take our order. Martin kept pelting him with rapid-fire questions, one after the other, and none of them serious. "Do you have a soup of the day? What about a soup of the month? Do you reuse the chili peppers from order to order, because they're so strong it's a shame to waste them? If we order the shark, will there be hands and feet inside?"

The waiter looked up, said "*Kew-zee me,*" put his pencil and pad in his pocket, turned on his heel, strode away from our table, across the dining room, and through the front door, where he stopped and looked up at the sky. The moon was, of course, full. I'll bet this happens to Martin a lot.

I myself never had to go outside and check the sky. When the first customer of the evening ordered "Steak tartare, well done," or "Geesh" I always knew we were witnessing the arrival of a strange visitor from another planet.

There is less humor but more variety in kitchen collectibles. Since necessity is the mother of invention, most kitchen implements are easily identifiable, and some are truly fascinating because of their narrow, specific uses. And food is such a basic need, people seem to gravitate toward items associated with food preparation, decoration, and consumption.

One area of collecting that will never lose its popularity is *automobilia,* or antiques and collectibles relating to cars, trucks, and other vehicles. Driving is such a major part of our lives, it's no wonder we're fascinated with vehicles, their origins, and all their accoutrements.

He Who Is The Light Of My Life and I, sometimes in the company of friends, have an amusing pastime that consists of trying to pin down the exact description of the Worst Driver on the Road.

My late father and I began this discussion years ago, and it has lasted for decades. We are like the old philosophers sitting under the olive trees in ancient Greece, attempting to reach a consensus on the exact nature of spiritual love. This could take forever.

When the discussion first started, we were not as sophisticated as we are today, so we began by establishing that the Worst Driver on the Road was always the Other Guy. This basic fact has never changed. It's the one truth we can count upon.

We started out simply, naming candidates such as elderly guys, men in hats, and doctors. For a while, the undisputed Worst Driver on the Road was the guy who drives with his arm hanging down out of the open window, sort of like he's wearing the car instead of sitting in it. Wives of doctors from New Jersey held the title briefly, as did all drivers with license plates that begin with "T" and end with "C" (livery cab drivers in New York City). Currently, private garbage-collection truck drivers are strong contenders, with ambulette drivers a close second (pretty scary thought, isn't it?).

No matter which type of driver causes you to wince when you meet him on the road, it's a safe bet that there's something about cars, new or classic, that attracts your eye and that you'd love to collect. The tips and tricks in this section are about caring for various materials. These formulas can be used on any of your collectibles, as long as they're made of the appropriate material. You should, of course, test a small, inconspicuous place on your item before you try any treatment on the whole object.

Dented Beer Cans

Puff out those dented cans. Beer-can collectors know that the dented ones are really cheap because nobody wants them. You can turn a dented can into a more valuable undented one.

Fill a dented can three-quarters full with dried peas. Pour water in, up to the top, seal the opening with a piece of tape, and let stand. When the peas absorb the water, they'll push the dents in the can outward.

Candles and Candleholders

To get wax off your candleholders, put them into the freezer for 15 minutes. When you take them out, the wax will break right off.

This candlestick was quickly cleaned of all wax drippings by placing it in the freezer.

To keep candles from dripping onto the candleholders in the first place, put your candles into the freezer for an hour. They'll never drip again.

LEATHER LORE

CLEAN YOUR vintage leather purses and belts with toothpaste. It's slightly abrasive and can be rubbed on with a soft cloth. Wipe off with a damp cloth.

Leather can also be cleaned with Turtle Wax Emerald Series Advanced Liquid Wax, the same kind used for cleaning cars. Apply with a cloth, wipe off with a damp cloth, then buff with a dry cloth. You may want to protect leather against scuffs with a coat of paste wax.

MARBLE MAGIC

MARBLE IS one of the trickiest materials to take care of. To keep your antique marble looking lovely, deal with any spills or stains promptly. You can make any stain disappear more quickly by warming the marble first. Use a blow dryer on the medium setting to do this.

- **Spots.** Sprinkle on baking soda and rub with a damp cloth.

- **Scratches.** Make a paste of baking soda and water. Apply and rub with very fine steel wool. Rinse with plenty of water and allow to dry. Buff with a dry cloth.

- **Water Stains.** Apply hydrogen peroxide with an eyedropper. Add a few drops of ammonia. Wait about half an hour, wash with clean water, and dry.

- **Other Stains.** Mix hydrogen peroxide with cream of tartar or regular (not gel) toothpaste. Rub in with a soft cloth, rinse, and dry.

Perfect Picture Frames

THE FIRST thing to remember is never place a piece of framed art flat on the table. If you drop something like your keys on it, or if your cat walks on it, or if your kid leans his elbow on it, you'll have a nice hole in the canvas.

When you acquire a framed picture, check that all the nails, staples, and other connectors are tight, secure, and free of rust. If not, replace them. Always replace the wire hanger unless you can tell that it's just been replaced. If you've ever had a picture fall off the wall in the middle of the night, you'll know why you should do this.

Many picture frames that look like carved wood are actually made of plaster, which can chip. You can do quick repairs on small chips using ordinary household spackling compound. Just mix according to the package directions (or use premixed spackle), and put a small amount on the chip. Add the spackle to the frame gradually, in layers, until the chipped spot is built up to the right height. Then use spackling tools, pins, nails, dental tools, your finger, or anything else that allows you to manipulate the moist spackle and duplicate the pattern on your frame. Let the spackle dry thoroughly, sand it, and paint it to match the rest of the frame.

To fill a small gouge, hole, or dent in the frame, you can pipe the spackling compound into position with a pastry bag (but never, ever use the bag for pastry again after that).

Most of the time, you should not do any more to your pictures than dust them and their frames with a dry, lint-free cloth. If you must clean paintings, try dabbing them with a piece of white bread or a slice of potato. If they don't come clean, take them to a professional.

Plastics

- **Cleaning.** Clean your plastic collectibles with baking soda on a damp sponge. Dry thoroughly.

- **Getting Odors Out.** If the object is polyethylene, put it in a box with crumpled newspapers and leave it overnight to remove unpleasant odors.

- **Polishing.** On polyethylene items, use a paste-type silver polish. On vinyl, use Pledge or paste wax.

Recipes and Newspaper Clippings

If you collect recipes but don't want a bunch of yellowing newspaper clippings hanging around, you can lift the print off the newspaper using wax paper and a knife. Place a sheet of wax paper, coated side down, over the recipe and rub with the dull edge of a knife blade to lift the recipe print; then place the wax paper on a clean piece of paper and rub again to complete the transfer.

If you prefer to keep the original clipping, here's a way to prevent the paper from yellowing and getting brittle. Dissolve a milk of magnesia tablet in a quart of club soda and let it stand overnight. Pour the solution into a pan large enough to hold your clipping. Soak the clipping in the pan for 1 hour. Remove and gently pat dry. Do not disturb until the paper is completely dry.

It is said that this formula will preserve a newspaper clipping for two hundred years. And who's going to be around to prove them wrong?

Treenware

TREENWARE IS the old-fashioned name for objects, especially kitchen items, made of wood. This name came from the plural of the word "tree," which used to be "treen."

Here are some helpful hints for cleaning and preserving your wooden kitchenware.

- **The Abrasive Lemon Method.** Because wood is porous, sometimes the best thing to do is eliminate the topmost layer of wood along with the dirt. You can do this with a half a lemon dipped in salt. Rub vigorously onto the wooden bowl or platter, rinse well, and dry thoroughly.

- **You Can Always Sand It.** Use fine-grit sandpaper so you don't remove too much wood. Wipe with a tack cloth or chamois, rinse well, and dry thoroughly.

- **Eliminating Odors.** Wet the wood and rub with dry mustard. Let stand for a few minutes, then rinse and dry thoroughly.

- **Now You Must Protect It.** The worst thing that can happen to beautiful wooden objects is for them to dry out, which may

Treenware is the old-fashioned name for kitchen objects made of wood.

cause them to crack. To prevent moisture loss, coat each piece with mineral oil. Be sure to use *edible* mineral oil on objects you're planning to use for food preparation or serving. Pour some oil onto a clean, soft cloth and rub it into the wood, going in the direction of the grain. Wipe off the excess with a paper towel. Wooden objects should be oiled periodically. Items that won't come in contact with food can be coated with paste wax.

A Final Word on the Tools of the Trade

- **Safe Socks.** Any procedure calling for a cloth is performed in my house with a sock. When a sock gets worn out, we never throw it away. We launder it and use it for cleaning. Socks fit neatly over the hand, and if they get really stained by some caustic solution, we can always throw them out. If you're concerned about solutions being absorbed through the sock and getting on your skin, wear a rubber glove under the sock.

Tools of the trade: socks, emery boards, and silica gel

- **Latex Gloves.** I use the disposable kind that can be purchased at hobby shops and medical-supply houses. When the job is done, I just strip them off and throw them away. They're not a great fit, but who cares?

- **Emery Boards.** I find emery boards so much better than sandpaper. They're easier to handle, they're sturdy, they get into tight places where sandpaper can't go, and each one comes equipped with a coarse-grit and a fine-grit side.

- **Silica Gel.** Those little packets of silica that come in the box with almost everything from cameras to vitamins are great for ensuring that humidity doesn't wreck your collectibles. I throw them in my jewelry trays, into closets and cabinets and drawers, and in with the silver, my cast iron, and other metals to prevent rust. Love 'em, and they're free.

- **Save Those Toothbrushes.** I never throw away an old toothbrush. Toothbrushes are great for getting into crevices, and they're easy to clean. They can even be used dry, to brush off surface dirt.

About the Author

JUDITH KATZ-SCHWARTZ was born and raised in New York City.

She began running a part-time antiques and collectibles business while working as an executive chef and corporate food executive. She founded Twin Brooks Antiques and Collectibles in 1986, and in 1987 she opened an independent appraisal practice. Since 1993, Judith has been doing business online, via her Twin Brooks Web site (www.msjudith.net).

Judith has been featured as a collectibles expert on numerous television and radio shows, among them FOX Television's top-rated FX cable network show *Personal FX: The Collectibles Show*, ABC's *Good Morning America*, NBC's *The Ainsley Harriott Show*, PAX TV's *Treasures in Your Home*, and *The Sally Jessy Raphael Show*.

She writes, edits, and publishes *The Antiques and Collectibles Newsletter*, an offbeat e-mail newsletter about collecting. She writes for *AntiqueWeek, Thompsons' Antiques Gazette, Unravel the Gavel*, and Ron McCoy's *Antiques & Collecting Newsletter*, and she speaks on collecting topics across the United States. Her articles are widely reprinted in the collecting press. Martingale & Company has twice called on Judith to serve as an expert contributor, for *Collector's Compass: Jewelry* and *Collector's Compass: Movie Collectibles*.

A member of Mensa, the International Society of Appraisers, the Association of Online Appraisers, the Ephemera Society of America, the Marble Collectors Society of America, and the Antiques and Collectibles Dealers Association, Judith also serves on the board of advisors of Collect-Tech, Inc., and is the moderator of the Collectibles & Memorabilia Forum on the *AntiqueWeek* Web site.

A serious collector of more things than she cares to ponder, Judith lives in Manhattan and Sullivan County, New York, with her husband, Arthur Schwartz, a computer expert.

Index

acetone, 60, 94
   See also nail-polish
      remover
acid, 49
alcohol, rubbing, 20,
   21, 37, 39
   and chrome, 58, 94
aluminum, 56, 58, 68,
   72, 87
ammonia, 37, 76,
   84–85, 106
ashes
   cigar, 31, 70
   wood, 61
Bakelite
   jewelry, 76
   radios, 94–96
baking soda, 107, 119,
   121
   and silver, 68, 70
   and toys, 22, 23, 25
Barbie dolls, 21
batteries, 25
beer cans, 118
bleach, 87, 103
blood, 109
brass, 56, 94
bread, 47, 48, 120
bronze, 57
burns, 109
cabbage, 61
candles, 32, 118
candle wax, 30
cast iron, 57, 124
cat litter, 55
chalk, 55, 71
charcoal, 55
chlorine, 57
chrome, 58, 94

cleaning
   dolls, 20–22
   furniture, 30–31
   glassware, 37–39
   jewelry, 76–78
   metals, 55–61, 67–70
   paper, 45–48
   porcelain, 84–85
   textiles, 102–109
Clearasil, 20, 21
coffee, 32
cola, 37, 55, 58, 85
cold cream, 31
copper, 59–61, 77–78
cornstarch, 37, 47, 48
cream of tartar, 84, 119
crystal, 39
denture powder, 22,
   38, 103
dolls, 17
   cleaning, 20–21
   repairing, 22
down, 111
drawers, sticking, 32
dust mites, 22
eggshells, 37–38
egg stains, 70
emery boards, 124
epoxy, 22
fabrics. *See* textiles
fabric softener liquid,
   68
fabric softener sheets,
   32, 46, 58
flour, 108
frames, 120
framing, 49
furniture, 27–32
   cleaning, 30–31

glassware, 34–39
glue, 95, 96
   and porcelain, 85–86
   removing, 30, 31, 48
gum, 30, 108
hairspray, 60
ink, 20, 108
jewelry, 74–80, 124
Jubilee kitchen wax,
   20, 21
ketchup, 23, 56, 78
knives, 56
lace, 105
lacquer, 59–60, 77–78
latex, 70–72, 124
leather, 119
lemon, 122
   and metals, 56, 60,
      94
   and silver, 69, 77
   and textiles, 104, 106
lighter fluid, 31, 48,
   93, 108
lipstick, 105
manure, 61
marble, 119
mayonnaise, 31
meat tenderizer, 109
metals, 51–61
microwaving, 46
milk, 20, 69, 86, 108
milk of magnesia, 121
mirrors, 37
mold, 20, 45–46
mothballs, 55, 72
moths, 102, 111
Mr. Clean, 76
music, 89–96
mustard, 39, 122

nail-polish remover, 21, 30, 58, 60, 94

newspaper, 37, 121

odors, 32, 45–46, 107, 121, 122

oil
  baby, 21
  lemon, 31
  mineral, 57–58, 123
  olive, 30, 31, 79
  salad, 31
  stains, 108

onions, 32, 56, 60

oven cleaner, 57

paint, on toys, 23

paper, 41–49

paraffin, 87

paste wax, 24, 94–95, 121, 123

peanut butter, 31

pearls, 79

peroxide, 84, 87, 105–106, 119

perspiration stains, 106

pewter, 61

pictures, 120

plastics, 23, 121

porcelain, 82–87

potatoes, 107, 120

pottery, 87

radios, 94–95

records, 93–94

repairing
  dolls, 22
  porcelain, 85–87
  radios, 95
  rugs, 107
  silver, 72
  toys, 24–25

rhinestones, 76, 79–80

rice, 38

rugs, 107–109

rust, 23, 84
  on fabrics, 104, 106
  on metals, 55–58
  on paper, 48
  preventing, 57–58

salt, 122
  and jewelry, 77–78
  and metals, 56, 60, 68, 94
  and textiles, 21–22, 104, 109

sandpaper, 122

scrapbooks, 42–45

shampoo, 77

shaving cream, 37, 108

silica gel, 124

silk, 99, 105–106

silver, 63–72
  cleaning, 68–70
  retarding tarnish, 70–71
  storage, 70–72

soap, 32

steel wool, 25, 67, 119

storage
  dolls, 22
  jewelry, 78, 80
  metals, 55, 70–72
  porcelain, 87
  records, 93
  textiles, 103, 109–111

Tang, 85

tea, 58, 84, 111

textiles, 98–111

toilet cleaner, 38

tomatoes, 77, 108

toothpaste, 31, 56, 70, 77, 119

Top Job, 76

toys, 16–25
  dating, 16–17
  stuffed, 22
  tin, 23–25
  vinyl, 25

treenware, 121–123

Vaseline Intensive Care lotion, 20

vegetable shortening, 20, 25

verdigris, 78

Victoria, queen of England, 28–29, 41–43

Victorian age
  scrapbooks, 42–45
  toys, 16

vinegar,
  and glassware, 37
  and jewelry, 77–78
  and metals, 25, 56, 58, 94
  and textiles, 103, 106–107

vinyl, 25

vodka, 37, 39

water, distilled, 39, 103–104

water stains, 31

wigs, 21

wine, 104, 105, 108

wood, kitchenware, 121–123

Worcestershire sauce, 60

World War II toys, 17